THAT'S **BS!**

How Bias Synapse Disrupts Inclusive Cultures
and the Power to Attract Diverse Markets

by

Risha D. Grant

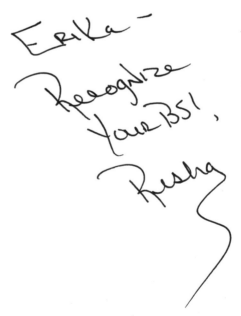

Erika —
Recognize
Your BS!,

Risha

First Printing, 2017

ISBN 978-0-9989944-0-6

F2 Publishing Group
P.O. Box 3131
Tulsa, OK 74101
www.RishaGrant.com

Dedication

This book is dedicated to "the others." The diverse people who have been ridiculed, afraid, hurt—physically and emotionally—but live their lives on their terms, anyway. You have given me the courage and freedom to live my life authentically.

TABLE OF CONTENTS

FOREWORD BY CARLTON PEARSON

"Prejudices are what fools use for reason." So says Voltaire, the French Enlightenment writer, historian, and philosopher who was famous for his wit and logic. More recently, the comedian W. C. Fields joked, "I am free of all prejudice. I hate everyone equally."

Prejudice is defined as a preconceived opinion that is not based on reason or actual experience. It comes from the Latin words for *before* and *judge* (*prae* + *judicium*): to judge before experiencing.

Seeing "BS" in the title of this book immediately grabbed my attention, simply because its hint of profanity created tension. We are conditioned to judge quickly, as though quick judgment were a life-and-death skill. Long ago, our survival literally depended upon our ability to respond quickly to tension. Today, we can use that skill for growth. Tension demands attention—which then creates the opportunity for intention. This book, written by my friend Risha Grant, is an educational tool for how to coexist on this planet authentically, respectfully, honestly, and with the dignity intrinsic to the highest expression of human nature.

She explains "bias synapse;" how our brains harbor bias in the deepest part of our subconscious. We unwittingly manifest our bias until we can identify, harness, and manage its influence on our actions. We all have biases and probably always will. Knowing this is the key to not allowing our biases to obstruct the accuracy of our perceptions, choices, and values. The word *synapse* is a derivative of the Greek word *synapsis*, which translates to "connection" or "junction." Deep inside all of us is a sense that this life is a connection to another one, either before or afterwards, indeed a junction between places, spaces, and spiritual paces.

Ultimately, life is a cause to which each of us is commissioned. We commit to surviving—and, I hope, also thriving. Yet we are also challenged along the way. Life in this earthly realm involves contact with races, religions, rites, rituals, and rules that spark inevitable tensions. As long as there are races, there will be varying levels of racism. And because we so often respond to difference in a subconscious, pre-judging way, racism and religion can be similar in their spiritual vibrations of prejudice and judgmentalism.

Amos 3:3 asks us, "How can two walk together except they be agreed?" The New International Version has it: "Do two walk together unless they have agreed to do so?" The Greek word for *agreement* is *symphoneo*, from which we also get the English word symphony. It doesn't mean that two things need to sound the same or even to sound alike. It just means to sound together. In other words, we don't have to go along to get along. We can mind many of the same things without having the same mind about everything. We must celebrate diversity rather than separate ourselves because of it.

In my book, *God Is Not a Christian, Nor a Jew, Muslim, Hindu*, there is a chapter titled, "What You Want, Wants You, Because What You Want *IS* You." Here is an excerpt from that chapter:

> The loneliest moment in your life is not when you lose friends, family or things. You are loneliest when you are away from, unaware of, or missing part of yourself... your own soul.
>
> You are most lonely and depressed when you have lost

your essence or forgotten who you are. Because of this or our spiritual amnesia, we have become transient souls, all but spiritual vagabonds seeking our own Self, our forgotten Self, the one we somehow and somewhere mislaid or misplaced, and in some cases, replaced with the impostor. Eckhart Tolle says in his book, *A New Earth*: "In the seeing of who you are not, the recognition of who you are, emerges."

In a sense, this book is Risha's official "coming out." She is owning and honoring her own truth after trying to play the role that society and the church expected, insisted, and all but demanded of her. As a rule, we humans spend most of our lives impersonating who we think people want us to be, and in the process, we disown and deny our authentic self and the honest and earnest realities incumbent on and within our humanness. We carry all of this into work daily and it affects our professional lives as well as our personal lives. Use Risha's personal anecdotes and client experiences to change the culture of your company through living authentically.

As you read my friend Risha's book, I encourage you to reclaim and reconnect to your essence—to your permanent rather than your accidental self. You will and should reconcile to the dignity, elegance, and eloquence of your essential Self. There is no greater freedom or joy in this human reality. Get ready for a journey to and through your inner BS You will come out a renewed person, able to refresh your self-experience and self-expression.

ACKNOWLEDGEMENTS

WOW! This book is finally finished. I have wanted to be an author since the second grade. I have talked about this book for the last ten years while finally starting and finishing it in 2013. This iteration is the second rewrite.

I've heard that writing a book is one of the loneliest endeavors a person can undertake. Although it did feel like that at times, I have had much help along the way. Hold on—this is about to sound like an acceptance speech at the Grammys.

First, I thank God for guidance on this project and the faith to know that my words will provide freedom not only for myself but also for others who walk a different path.

To the women in my life: I am eternally thankful for your guidance and love. Even if you are not mentioned by name, there are so many who have blessed me throughout my life.

First and foremost, all my love and appreciation to my grandmother, Ola Mae Knox. Her teachings through her life experiences were the premise for this book idea. Your role in my life is immeasurable, and I pray I have made you proud. I miss you daily.

My mother, Penny Grant-Edd. I am because of who you are. Your encouragement, the positive reinforcement, and the many conversations are all unmatched. I cherish your presence in my life daily. Thank you for loving me through my journey and allowing me to be me even when you didn't understand. Now that you do understand, you remind me of who I am and that it is okay for me to live authentically, even when I have forgotten.

My partner and fiancé, Carmela Hill. You are the wind beneath my wings and maybe the hurricane blowing me to kingdom come when I need a wake up call. I can't say enough about your patience throughout this process. I can't thank you enough for allowing me to bounce ideas off of you, day and night. I admire your intellect so much that when you are on board with an idea, I know it will be successful. These past ten years have helped me to see life differently and have greatly added to my personal growth. Your love and faith in me have carried me when the circumstances say otherwise.

My sister, Tasha Scott. My first best friend and ride-or-die partner. You were the first family member on this journey of self-discovery with me. I was able to breathe deeply and know that no matter what happens in this world, you would be by my side. You never lost a beat in allowing me to be me, and you fiercely protected me from anyone who tried to block that process. I learned more about unconditional love when you handed me my most important role with the births of my favorite niece (Kambry) and my favorite nephew (Koen). I can't imagine life without you in it.

Aunt Nay, you spoke nothing but success, love, and God into my life. You taught through humor and love but always kept it real. There was never a time when you didn't have just the right message to get me through a tough time. You have even appeared in my dreams to let me know you're still by my side. I always hear that little voice inside me that says, "No matter what it looks like, keep going." I know it's you.

Alaina Jones, I'm not sure where to begin. You started out as an employee but have become family. We have been through a lot in the past seven years, but you have stuck by my side through it all. There will never be words to adequately capture your loyalty and support of my vision. You have pushed me. You have disagreed with me (often), but it was all done with the end goal in mind. We have spent endless hours discussing the concepts for this book and working through my mind to get it all on paper. I truly don't have the words for what you mean to me personally and professionally. Thank you.

delmetria millener, I know you hate the mushy stuff, but I love you for pushing me to actually start this book. We talked about it forever and after lovingly cursing me out, we got the process started. You edited the first iteration and it about drove both of us crazy, but you will see our conversations and thoughts interwoven in my words. I appreciated the early morning discussions, the late night rants, and both of us telling each other off in order to put out the best product. Most importantly, I appreciate that our friendship is one that is blessed until the end of time.

Sarah Cypher, the kickass editor. You never missed a deadline, although I missed many. Your words, ideas, and guidance helped me get this book to print. I can't thank you enough. I hope you enjoyed the process as much as I did because we will be doing it again.

Alison Anthony, thank you, thank you, thank you. I asked you to read this book as a D&I practitioner but you went above and beyond. Your tidbits of insight made this book stronger and your thoughts about cursing gave me what I needed not to worry about it. Also, I'll be forever grateful that you took the time during a family birthday celebration to discuss your thoughts.

To the main guy in my life, my dad, Lawrence (Peanut) Grant. You haven't always understood what I was doing with my career or my business, but it didn't matter because you encouraged me every step of the way. When I call you upset, you always say, "Baby, Daddy doesn't know what you are talking about, but we will figure it out." Somehow, that always brings me comfort, because you are there. Your love and support have given me security and a sense of self. Thank you for being there.

To the people that read the first iteration of this book (Cathy, Sarah, and Mitzi), thank you for still choosing to be my friends. It was a tough read.

If you were not mentioned by name but feel you should be, please charge it to my head and not my heart. I am truly blessed to have so many people walk through this journey with me—to include them all would be a book in itself.

INTRODUCTION

I'm a small-town, divorced, ex-preacher's wife. I come from a loving and largely religious family. To the world, I am a competitive, relentless, ex-division-one-basketball player— and to my friends, I am an extremely loyal but conditional extrovert. I also happen to be a bisexual black woman, a serial entrepreneur, and a Catholic-middle-school basketball coach who runs a diversity communications and consulting firm in the "reddest" state in the nation.

I am diversity personified. So are you.

Also, are you ready? I didn't trust white people. I don't fully understand why girls want to be boys and boys want to be girls, and I cannot stand organized religion. That is not all. I used to struggle with accepting interracial relationships. I use the word nigga even though I know it denigrates my community, but I feel disrespected by anyone outside of the black community who uses it.

Like you, I formed my biases through life experiences. I have worked to admit that I have biases that have sometimes affected my life, both personally and professionally. Even though I may not understand or even like some things about other people, I know that I cannot judge them or treat them less kindly for it. Everyone deserves respect—no exceptions. You've heard of the Golden Rule: to treat others as you want to be treated. That's a pretty easy concept, isn't it? And without making it too complicated, we can do even better than that. Let's strive for the "Platinum" Rule: to treat others as they want to be treated.

Let me take a pause to lay the framework for how we use

words in this book and in my business. Don't be over-sensitive! People are already uptight about diversity. If we put too much emphasis on political correctness, we will never get anywhere. For example, I prefer the word black over African American but I won't go ballistic about it. The words transgender and transsexual are interchangeable in most contexts. The same is true of gay, homosexual, and lesbian. You might use the term minority when referring to anyone outside of the "Caucasian" or

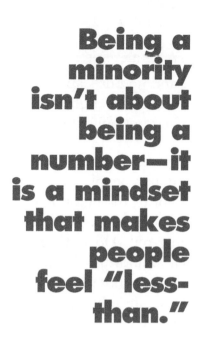

Being a minority isn't about being a number—it is a mindset that makes people feel "less-than."

"white" population. However, I dislike the word minority because, by definition, it means "a racial, ethnic, religious, or social subdivision of a society that is subordinate to the majority group in political, financial, or social power without regard to the size of these groups."[1] That being said, I consider myself an ambassador for "minorities" to be treated equally and inclusively so they can live as they please in this world. At the end of the day, I don't like the term, but I don't care if others use it.

Anyone who gets upset about words like these will shut down interactions and promote separation. If you use words like

---

1 "minority." Dictionary.com. Dictionary.com Unabridged. Random House, Inc. http::www.dictionary.com/browse/minority (accessed: January 24, 2017).

nigga, wetback, faggot, or dyke, though—we have a serious problem that has nothing to with political correctness. These words are hateful, and they spew disrespect. We are who we are, and no one's approval is needed. Everyone should have that inalienable right. When someone doesn't have that right, it affects not only them, but you, too.

Being a minority isn't about being a number—it is a mindset that makes people feel "less-than." When people are *treated* as a minority, the emotional consequences can show up as low productivity at work, low self-esteem, or even some form of lashing out. Do not lump diverse people under the single label, "minorities." Each is a diverse individual who has a voice and whose contributions have inspired and catapulted America into the number-one economy in the world. We all deserve equal access to schools, healthcare, careers, and homes. I am working to do my part to make a difference. So should you be.

MY STORY

Inequality has wreaked havoc across the nation since the beginning of its days. In the late 1990s, I set out to balance the scales of justice. I started my company focused on creating awareness for black-owned businesses to sell their products and services in mainstream markets. As my business grew, I saw the value of working with all diverse markets. I positioned my company to respond to this increased opportunity. For fifteen years, I tried to convince companies of the need to invest in diversity and inclusion (D&I). At first, I made little progress. Today, I have learned, reinvented, and sustained my efforts so I could continue to hone my craft while educating others on D&I's benefits. Consistently, I remind companies that attracting diverse customers to their products and services, and recruiting and retaining a diverse workforce can and does positively affect their company's economic strength.

I have been asked more times than I can count how I got into this line of work. The more I think about it, I realize that I didn't pick it; it picked me. I now think of it as some divine interlude that introduced me to my purpose in life.

One of my favorite quotes is from Mark Twain: "The two most important days of your life are the day you were born and the day you find out why."

There were multiple days, which led me to finding my life's "why."

One of my defining moments took place on a family road trip to Gadsden, Alabama when I was fourteen. I remember three things about that trip. (1) We passed by the Piggly Wiggly where (I thought) a scene from *Driving Miss Daisy* was filmed. I wanted to go inside and take a picture, but my parents would not stop. (2) When we finally arrived in Gadsden, it was at the height of summer. Whenever someone says "burning in hell," Gadsden is the first place that comes to mind. It is the hottest place I have ever been. The heat was a problem because this was the era of playing outside; adults would kick you out of the house and not let you back in, especially for something as trivial as being hot. (3) It was apparent to me that black people were running this city. They probably were not, but in my fourteen-year-old mind, they were.

When my cousins and I watched TV, the actors in most commercials were black people, and they were promoting black businesses and products. I even saw a commercial for a black doll! As we were driving down the street, we passed a billboard featuring a black family. Before visiting this sweatbox, I had never noticed the fact that there were so few black people on my TV set at home. I was in awe and wondered for the first time why I never saw toys that looked like me on my TV at home. I had grown accustomed to my reality and didn't realize I was deprived.

The more things change, the more they stay the same. By 1997, there were a lot more black people acting in national commercials, and it was no longer an anomaly to see blacks on TV. Local television, however, had not changed that much since I visited Gadsden. I decided to do something about it. I focused my business development on African American businesses located in North Tulsa (the area of our city mostly populated by African Americans) because I wanted to highlight the city's diverse businesses. I set out to make television commercials affordable for small black businesses. As my new business grew, I started to dabble in some aspects of public relations—producing marketing materials led to writing and distributing press releases. I loved public relations and felt I had the personality for it.

As I researched how to make a living through entrepreneurship, I found Tulsa inundated with PR and marketing firms. I kept asking myself, *How can my small firm compete?* One night I was in one of my favorite places, the local Barnes & Noble bookstore, trying to soak up more knowledge and find just the right business books. I love to read, so I decided to look at a few fiction titles, too, and there—in the middle of all these novels—was the answer to the question that was lodged in my brain: a business book on multicultural marketing, mis-shelved among the store's African American novels. Divine intervention.

I bought the book and went straight home to start working on my business. I was twenty-two years old; young enough to think I knew everything and bold enough to try almost anything. Since that year, my PR firm has been the only firm in the state of Oklahoma to focus on diversity communications. Back then, it was a great way to break into the local market because no one—absolutely no one—specialized in this niche.

In my research, I came across an article in *Advertising Age* that talked about the trend among major advertising and public relations firms to buy into smaller firms operating in the African American, Hispanic, and LGBTQ markets. For instance, in 2013, McCann Worldwide created a partnership with the Hispanic agency Casanova to form McCann Casanova. Together they launched a health marketing unit to increase their pharma contracts. Big firms were gobbling up at least half the ownership in these companies because they realized that demographics were changing rapidly, and diverse consumer markets broadened the consumer base and increased their clients' revenue.

By the time I read about it in *Advertising Age*, I had been trying for a few years to introduce diverse businesses to the Tulsa customer base. To that end, this article carried the arsenal of information I needed to blast onto the scene. I ordered up a boost of confidence to match my awesome presentation. My plan was to march into the largest firms in Tulsa to let them know that they needed to add a multicultural division to their firms, and that I needed to be in charge of it. To any firm that showed interest, I requested partial ownership in their firms. After all, I was going to be building this massive division to access these new, diverse markets.

My plan had a couple of major flaws. First, no one really knew who I was. Second, no one knew my skill set well enough to consider my proposal. Most of the firms humored me and listened. Now I realize that was a success in itself. Graciously, one executive in particular allowed me to make a presentation to his entire firm, including its partners. Today, I cringe when I think about that horrible presentation. This was long before I ever became a public speaker. I showed no personality. I was sweating a lot and threw out many rapid-fire stats about why they should be interested in diverse markets. Everyone seemed to be staring at me with a look that said, Please die a quick death so we can get out of this damn meeting. I believe their majority partner was very interested in my idea, but knew the market much better than I did. He understood that regardless of whether you could show verified stats and beautiful demographic charts, it was going to take a lot longer for decision-makers to change their mindset and open their wallets for diverse consumers.

Here is where I got my feelings hurt. I went to another large media firm and made my presentation to their CEO. I had heard that he was a difficult man and could be harsh, but what did I have to lose? I entered the room locked and loaded; I rehearsed and was ready to blast him with the sweetest presentation he had ever heard. Throughout my entire presentation, he did not say a word. He flipped back and forth through the written presentation, which was still a lot better than my verbal one. When I finished, awkward silence engulfed the room.

He asked, "Do you really think anybody here cares about diversity? This is Oklahoma."

It was brutally honest, but in hindsight, he probably just said what everyone from the other presentations was thinking.

I was pissed off. I began to ramble off the U.S. Census

population predictions again, but it was useless. As I turned to leave, feeling rejected and a little stupid, he asked if he could keep my presentation material. Later, I cheered myself up by thinking that he must have seen some value in it since he wanted to keep my information.

Although no one took me up on my audacious idea, I was arrogant enough to think that these companies simply did not know a good idea when they heard one. As I look back now, the idea was way before its time. Oklahoma demographics nor our business climate was strong enough for multicultural marketing to be a viable option. However, I still think that if any of these firms had the foresight to predict how we could have worked together, it would have increased the bottom line for all of us, especially at a time when no one in Oklahoma was even thinking about diversity as an economic engine. I am certain that these firms' clients would have been better served if they'd received a complete communications plan that included diverse audiences. If developed and executed properly, that plan would have improved their bottom line while setting them up for future growth.

It took a while for my head to catch up with my heart, but I am glad that none of those firms were interested in my idea. I get to claim my success as my own.

I currently own Risha Grant LLC. We are the only award-winning, full-service diversity communications, consulting, recruitment, and training firm in Oklahoma. It has been no small feat, building a diversity and inclusion firm in one of the most conservative states in the nation. If it were not for my family, I may have starved. There were times when the challenges didn't seem worth it. But today, we have managed to become a multi-million-dollar company.

As I said earlier, I did not choose this industry—it chose me.

This book is a culmination of the past eighteen years of my experiences in running a D&I company. Many people I have encountered along my journey hold the misconception that D&I is complex and costly. In fact, it's simple and adds to the bottom line. I always share with my clients that the cost of inclusion is a lot cheaper than the cost of exclusion. D&I is only costly when you spend hard-earned profits on lawsuits or court-appointed mandates. Otherwise, it is a necessary business expense to make sure you provide your employees with a work environment conducive to producing the best products and services. If you meet this basic need, you will realize that your employees will, in turn, feel like a valued member of the team. You will receive the best they have to offer, and this will show in your bottom line.

This book is divided into two parts. Part I will focus on bias, as it is the root cause of most diversity and inclusion issues. My research will explain how our brains process bias and I will provide you with the keys to address bias within yourself and others. Part II applies the lessons of Part I to your organization's internal operations, and will focus on building an inclusive culture through recruiting and retaining diverse employees. It further turns that work outward, focusing on attracting diverse customers. You will also notice Permission: Granted tips at the end of each chapter. Many times, we don't give ourselves permission to work on our inner feelings. I'm granting you permission through those tips to get in where you fit in.

A lot of deep-dive research exists to support these benefits, but I will not dig into the comprehensive, analytical research of numbers or share a colorful discussion of the social ills that degrade America's race relations, expression of identity, household wealth, and education—or how inequality undercuts our society's potential for maximum prosperity. The basic concept of diversity and inclusion is simple, and so is this book.

Here's a fact: history is full of pain and inequality. It falls to each of us to learn about the events that haunt our fellow citizens—the Holocaust for Jews, slavery for blacks, land theft for Native Americans, internment for Japanese Americans, and more. Real injustices have laid the foundation for racism and suspicion. Yet I work in the gray area between recognizing difference and just respecting everyone equally. I've seen how the simple concept of respecting each other sometimes gets lost in the details of all this history. In missing the forest for the trees, people become jaded or feel blame and turn off to embracing the humanity in each other because competing narratives dredge up painful feelings on all sides. It is validated pain, but it is still pain that keeps us living in an us-versus-them world. This pain keeps us from acceptance and openness.

As adults, we are all responsible for ourselves and we owe it to each other to get out of our own way and fix our internal BS so that we coexist respectfully. Let's learn about that BS now.

PART I: BIAS

CHAPTER 1
COMPANIES DON'T HAVE DIVERSITY PROBLEMS

If a career such as mine exists, the world is f—k'd up.

For eighteen years, I have been running an award-winning diversity communications and consulting firm in one of the reddest states in the nation. In the last presidential election, not one of the seventy-seven counties had a majority who voted for the Democratic candidate. Our main service is to bridge the gap between mainstream and diverse communities by helping our clients attract diverse customers to their products and services. Over half of Oklahoma's population falls into a diverse category, and those categories don't include women, LGBTQ individuals, or specific religions. You would think that we have no choice but to interact with all varieties of people, but that is not the case. There are many times that I am still the only black person in the room. I am in meetings all the time, constantly pushing an agenda of diversity and inclusion. I have sat on boards where I'm continually asked how to get the diverse crowds involved in events or how to get diverse people to patron attractions. Many times, however, I have to prove it can be done.

For instance, my firm hosted a party for a club whose membership was thinning: in part due to old age, but also because it was a good ol' boy network. We hosted a "Black Out" party. Our goal was to help our client create awareness of the club and generate more memberships. We had a jazz band, an R&B band, a hip-hop DJ, and a rock band. Everyone came out. To this day, it is still one of the most diverse parties our city has ever seen. The people who attended to hear the jazz band taught some of the hip-hop people how to dance. It was truly a fun night that represented all the kinds of people who live in our city. It proved that we could get along and have fun together. People still ask me about that event and it was 10 years ago.

In other words, it can be done. Diversity exists all around us, right now. Our clients want to cash in on the trillions of dollars in disposable income from diverse consumers, or they want to establish their brand as one that embraces diversity and inclusion. Since I started working in this industry, I have experienced three evolutions of the D&I paradigm and the related obstacles that we still have to clear. Let's review the landscape.

LEVELS OF DIVERSITY AND INCLUSION

1. Affirmative Action

Executive Order 10925 was signed by President John F. Kennedy in 1961. It stated that government entities were required to implement policies, guidelines, and administrative practices to end and correct discrimination in government-sanctioned and government-mandated education and hiring. Many companies also put their own policies in place, and affirmative action was born. The order provided special consideration to historically excluded groups, such as people of color and women.

During this time, "minority contracting" became commonplace; in other words, a percentage of contracts are awarded to minority-owned vendors. The newer term for this is supplier diversity. Of course, the practice did not go over well. To many in the white community, affirmative action is reverse discrimination. The good ol' boy network hated this. They felt that it excluded white males. A commonly held belief among white people was this: there is a white candidate and person of color up for one position. When reviewing resumes, the white person is more qualified for the position. Due to affirmative action, however, the person of color gets hired because the box needs to be checked. The white community felt as if affirmative action lowered their standards. I began working in D&I as states were starting to repeal affirmative action. Yep, you guessed it; Oklahoma was one of the states who succeeded in doing so.

Of course, research had justified the strong need for affirmative action as a remedy: out of billions of dollars in government contracts, women only received around 2.5 percent. African American and Hispanic median households still earn almost $20,000 less than Caucasian households do, and they lag in every category from education and income to employment and healthcare.

Take Walmart for example. In a 2003 study by University of California-Hayward professor Dr. Richard Drogin, he discovered that women made up 72 percent of Walmart's total workforce but only 33 percent of its managers. These numbers led Walmart to court—as the defendant in a national gender-bias lawsuit. To add insult to injury, even today it really sucks that women who earn their master's degree still make less than men who have an undergraduate degree.

Leveling the playing field is difficult but less problematic than allowing these inequities to remain unaddressed. The reality is that qualified, diverse people are overlooked all the time in hiring for ridiculous reasons. In the case of women and non-white applicants, there can be unrealistically high expectations. In some cases, if all else is equal, a SHE would not be hired because she is "pushy and abrasive" while a HE would be hired because those same traits come across as "assertive and bold" to the biased eye.

2. Social Justice

There was no executive order or mandate for social justice. As affirmative action waned, people tried to appeal to the humanity in others. D&I practitioners pleaded for corporate citizenship as a way to break through to human resource departments. This is where we began to see companies embrace Taco Tuesday and Black History Month programs.

I started my business during this era. I would inform potential clients that embracing diversity and inclusion was just "the right thing to do." Businesses, however, could not grasp the social justice viewpoint because I didn't articulate a business case for it. In retrospect, it is unsurprising that my approach got no traction. I was not speaking about diversity and inclusion as an economic engine. Businesses typically spend money to make money, and "conscious-capital" organizations were rare during this time.

3. Competitive Advantage

This paradigm shift (along with US Census numbers) changed the game. I understood quickly that I needed to readjust my sales pitch and that using the words "competitive advantage" piqued interest among decision-makers. This was the business case that I needed to break through to clients.

Do not get me wrong—inclusion is the right thing to do for its own sake. But every company is looking for an advantage over the next one. Competitive advantage pairs the economic engine with the real value of diversity and inclusion. Finally, I got back to the reason it all made sense to me in the beginning. The commercials I saw in Gadsden, Alabama reflected the community that lived there. The population was over 30 percent African American, and businesses would have passed up a lot of money had they only marketed to Caucasians. But only now are today's big companies catching up with that idea. For instance, the New York Times ran an article in 2016 stating that three large companies—Verizon, HP, and General Mills—sent letters to their ad agencies asking how many women and minorities they had on staff and what their action plans were for increasing those numbers.

Verizon's letter described diversity as an "explicit business imperative." The letter further stated that "we are more likely to create solutions that amaze our customers if our work force and suppliers represent the communities we serve." Large companies are encouraging D&I by publicly demanding that ad agencies diversify their employees or lose their business.

Now that we've talked about the three stages of D&I's evolution, let's bring it back to your own workplace. Does your company or organization embrace D&I, or does it regard D&I with suspicion? Based on my experience, how

If a career such as mine exists, the world is f—k'd up.

work colleagues deal with diverse employees, a diverse person, or a D&I practitioner will usually be predicted by not only their own experiences but also by the era in which D&I was introduced to them and under what circumstances. I am asked a lot how to get D&I buy-in from executives.

This is where it's important to understand the evolutions of the D&I paradigm. If you are working with someone who understands diversity and inclusion from the affirmative action era, they may not be as open to or accepting of policies and procedures that embrace D&I. You will have to work harder to convince them of its importance. Someone from the era of competitive advantage typically understands it is a business imperative. Try to be conscious of who you are dealing with as you present D&I to your company.

FOUR TYPES OF D&I COMPANIES

When I think of the different types of organizational attitudes toward D&I, interestingly, they lend themselves to metaphors I borrow from organized religion.

The Choir

These are companies that fully embrace diversity and inclusion and understand its value. Selling them on D&I is like preaching to the choir.

I love these companies. They have communicated their vision vividly to all employees—from the CEO down to entry-level positions. It is evident when looking at the company's website that its core values include diversity and inclusion. These companies are proactive regarding any issue surrounding D&I. They usually have a zero-tolerance policy for bullshit.

The Disciples

These companies are eager to learn about D&I. They know they need it but may not know where to start. They seek out coaching, they ask questions, and they research all they can. Once they get it, they have no problem with implementation and execution. I love to work with this type of company. They are open, inquisitive, and seek to build the best company and culture within their power.

The Agnostics

These companies doubt the possibility that D&I is an integral part of business, so they aren't yet ready to put any resources toward it. They know they need to do it. They have probably had personnel or customer issues, but they wouldn't call it a "problem." This kind of company is most worrisome because they will not understand it's a problem until they pay out millions in a lawsuit. These companies waste my time. They arrange endless meetings and want me to tweak my proposal fifty-eleven times (fifty-eleven is slang for a lot), but they never move forward.

Nonbelievers

These companies were sued for millions of dollars, damaging their reputation. Still, they do not believe that D&I is imperative to business success. Everything they do regarding D&I is forced and reactive. They do not understand the value, but they comply to avoid further lawsuits and more deterioration of their reputation. These are the hardest clients to work with. They do not value the work, diversity, or inclusion. They are checking off a box so they are not sued again. I've found that typically, it makes little sense to work with these clients in the absence of an ally, because at worst it can hurt your reputation and in the least it will definitely frustrate the hell out of you.

After experiencing every level of evolution in various companies and working to understand where they fall on the D&I spectrum, I can truly say this: Companies don't have diversity problems. They have people problems.

DIVERSITY

Companies usually hire me in a reactive mode to "fix" their diversity problems. In and of itself, that is the problem. Diversity cannot be fixed. It just is. It is our race, ethnicity, physical abilities, socioeconomic status, age, sexual orientation, religion, and gender. It is also our food preferences, thought processes, clothing choices, how we rock our hairstyle, our political beliefs... I could go on and on, but it is who we are. Point blank. Period.

What diversity is not is something that needs to be fixed or that needs approval from others. This kind of thinking is what causes the issues in the first place. When we don't understand each other or agree with another person's lifestyle or identity, we communicate in unspoken ways that he or she has lost some of our respect. Remember, diversity and inclusion is a simple goal! You do not have to understand me to show me common courtesy. I said at the beginning of this chapter that if a job like mine exists, the world is f—ed up. It is because as humans, we have forgotten our humanity, our respect, and our common courtesy. I spend most of my time reminding adults of the manners they learned as children: respect others, work well with others, avoid name-calling because it is hurtful (and expensive), be fair, and share.

Companies don't have diversity problems.

They have people problems.

I have spent more than half of my career educating people, although it felt more like begging them at times. I am passionate about wanting people to see and understand the importance of diversity and inclusion to their workforce and community. Unfortunately, what has happened is that I have sometimes become the one who is disgusted with people. Shocking? Allow me to retract. In all fairness, what exhausts me is the process, but it feels like it is the people because when the process is all about dismantling bias that real people uphold, it is easier to blame the people. I have what I call McDonald's days. These are the days when I would like to go and cook fries at McDonald's. I would like to do my shift and go home. I don't want to discuss the fries. I don't want to fix the bad fries. I would like to do my job, go home, and not think about the fries until my next shift. I can't do that with this career that has chosen me. I have to keep fighting. I have to keep getting up and having the same conversations that I have had for years with the same people about the same damn topic. Equality is important. It is worth the fight.

I had to go through my own process to realize that what frustrated me was about more than lack of respect; I had much

Diversity cannot be fixed. It just is.

deeper-rooted issues at work in the core of myself. So do you. It all happens in our brains—it's called bias, and it is BS.

INCLUSION

Ultimately, the goal is to create value around people's differences so they have permission to be themselves. People are happiest and most productive when they are able to reveal authenticity. If you have tried to be anyone other than yourself, you can understand the self-loathing this causes. Diversity focuses on our differences. It's not a bad thing, but it is the part of the D&I dynamic that separates us. Without it, our lives would resemble The Stepford Wives. Therefore, we cannot talk about diversity without talking about inclusion.

Inclusion is the other part of the D&I dynamic. It brings us together and makes us stronger. Diversity is about you; inclusion is about us. Inclusion makes your diverse workforce jell. It helps you make better products. It provides better solutions and it enhances services. Why? Because people with different life experiences and from different backgrounds are bringing their unique perspectives to the table and creating the magic that increases your revenue, your brand, and your reputation.

You don't have a choice in diversity, but you create opportunity with inclusion. Yes, I said it. You do not have a choice when it comes to diversity. Be real, open your eyes, and look around you. Hiring diverse people is the new normal. For those of you who are not surrounded by people who look different from you, allow me to introduce you to the new world. For the first time, the United States currently has five different generations in the workforce at the same time. Ninety-two percent of the US population growth is due to ethnic groups and the U.S. Census Bureau predicts that the US will become "minority majority" by 2044. The National Gay and Lesbian Taskforce estimates 3–8 percent of the American population is gay, but the Gallup Poll shows numbers as high as 21 percent for men and 22 percent for women. Whether we have the exact number or not, it fair to say that you are in fact working with or living next to someone from the LGBTQ community. So, even for those who are intentionally or unintentionally practicing bias in hiring, you will eventually run out of options.

Do not get me wrong! I'm not saying that diverse hiring practices will someday be automatic so therefore you don't need to worry about it. I am letting you know that as demographics continue to change, our world is becoming more and more diverse. Choosing diversity is becoming less of a choice. It will be the new normal. You should be asking yourself by now, How do I achieve inclusion? You do it by being intentional.

Here is the perfect example. As a kid, my older cousins forced me to play basketball with them almost daily so they would have enough players. However, they would hardly ever let me touch the ball, and no one worried about guarding me. It was as though I were invisible. They had to have me, per the rules of the game, but they didn't allow me to participate. As the smallest and youngest of the bunch, I began to accept my own fate that they would continue to make me play. I had no voice and brought no value to them other than being a token body. If I touched the ball, they quickly yelled at me to pass it to someone else.

THIS IS NOT INCLUSION

In other words, just because you allow someone on the court does not mean they automatically get to play, and just because you hire a diverse individual does not mean they actually get to contribute or feel like a valued member of the team. Someone has to allow that person's voice to be heard, receive their ideas, and actually implement one or two of them from time to time when the ideas are good. To be a part of the team, at some point, someone has to put the ball in your hands.

When I interview a client's employees, I am often told by diverse individuals that they always feel they need to prove their worthiness to other team members when working on a project. They feel the need to prove they are worthy to perform the job they were hired to do. As a D&I practitioner who was once an undervalued little girl on the court, I understand in my bones what they're saying.

After being forced to be a token body in my cousins' games, I began to practice on my own. I was practicing because I was tired of my cousins never allowing me to touch the ball. It was not because I liked the sport. I was on a mission to prove my worthiness. Another cousin who saw me practicing became my advocate. Without him, there was no way a kid my age, my gender, and my skill level would have ever gotten the respect of being allowed to play with the boys who took over the gym around 6 p.m. every night. Much to the chagrin of the other players, my older cousin would pick me to be on his team. He would coach me during the game, pass me the ball, and block the other players so I was allowed to shoot and dribble.

THIS IS INCLUSION

He didn't just let me be on his team. He included me. He let me play. He gave me room to make mistakes, he worked with me on my weak areas, and he told the other players to shut up and leave me alone. I actually began to like basketball. I was able to prove to my other cousins and everyone else that I was worthy to be a part of the game. This experience parlayed into a sports career that won me a full scholarship to play division-one basketball in college. I thrived in the game. Can your employees thrive in their field of play?

Inclusion is intentional. It translates into value, and your diversity only matters in the sense that it is your competitive edge. If you ever want to make a difference in someone's life, you will do that through inclusion. It makes you a part of their success.

PERMISSION: GRANTED TO

- Be an inclusive advocate for someone else by creating opportunities for them to grow and contribute.

- Always remember that D&I is simple. Be careful not to lose the simplicity of humanity in all of the emotion.

- Understand that companies don't have diversity problems. They have people problems. You are the problem. We are the problem. It's on all of us to fix it.

- Remind yourself and others that diversity is not a problem that needs to be fixed. Diversity is a pathway to inclusion. Diversity is about you; inclusion is about us.

CHAPTER 2

I MIGHT BE A RACIST

The elements that make us different—race, religion, age, economics, gender, physical ability, sexuality, and more—are the very fibers of our identity.

They give us our cool factor. At work, at home, at school, at church, and in social settings, they influence our reactions to and relationships with other people.

Once I settled into my career in diversity communications, my own fibers began to announce themselves louder with each new project and every new client. So much so, I had to step back and examine their impact on how I lived and worked, on everything and everyone around me. Inevitably, I realized something was off.

In 2009, when I decided to merge my diversity communications firm with another PR firm that was white-owned, I figured out what was off. It was me. I was racist.

It was an interesting time for my firm. The Tulsa World named me one of four upcoming people to watch in the community and business realm. I raised $250,000 toward improving the image of the area where most of Tulsa's African American community lived. The initiative created media attention for my firm, and we were hired to work alongside another PR firm to garner diverse community input for a huge city project. As we worked together, we started to flirt with the idea of merging our firms. Publicly, we moved forward. There were press releases and articles on our merger. Essentially, a white-owned firm was finally recognizing what I had seen ten years earlier—a real opportunity to grow business through diverse markets. Talk about coming full circle.

A little while after I moved into my new partner's office, I had to have a surgical procedure. I was supposed to be out two weeks, but due to complications, I was out for six. During the transition of the merger, I let most of my staff go except for one part-time person. I was handling all of my clients. As the weeks turned into a month, I was distraught. Could I maintain my client base?

My new partner told me to send him my list of clients, their contact information, and what needed to be done. I dragged my feet for weeks. Instead, I opted to call and discuss what was going on with each client and asked for a grace period while I got back on my feet. Frustrated, my new partner wondered why I declined his help. I really had no answer. As more weeks passed, a friend asked me why I didn't let my partner take some of the stress off. After all, what was the use in having a partner if I hoarded my workload?

Offhandedly and with so much ease, I said, "Girl, I do not trust that white man with my clients. He will probably have stolen all of them by the time I get back into the office."

Fast-forward a year. I was meeting with a bank executive about the possibility of working with them on a diversity and inclusion (D&I) initiative. By the fifth ninety-minute meeting, she still didn't understand the need for embracing D&I. She said, "Give me one word that will sell this to my boss."

I wasn't racist, but I recognized that I had a definite bias.

I said, "lawsuit."

I went back to my office, frustrated and perplexed by her lack of understanding. There is something wrong with these people, I kept thinking. D&I is a simple concept. There had to be something there, internally, that continued to hold them back. I thought that if I could figure out what that was, I would hit the jackpot.

It took me a long time—four years, to be exact. In 2013, I was preparing for my first national speech and going through a rebranding process for my company. I needed to do some introspection and spend a lot of time thinking through diversity, inclusion, my voice, and my clients' needs. I was lying on the floor in my home office thinking over my years in business. I wondered why diversity and inclusion was such a hard sell. Why did I keep having the same conversations year after year? Then I started to look internally. I'm very big on faith and the Law of Attraction, which is the ability to draw what you want into your life simply by focusing on it. I started to think about how this work truly made me feel, and everything became clear. I did not trust white people. The longer I thought about it, I began to think that maybe I was racist. Imagine the panic that began to permeate my body. This couldn't be right! I'm a diversity and inclusion consultant, for God's sake! I teach companies how to embrace D&I and I have many white friends whom I genuinely love. I grabbed my phone, went to Dictionary.com, and looked up the word racist.

"A person who believes in racism, the doctrine that one's own racial group is superior or that a particular racial group is inferior to the others."

Whew! I wasn't racist, but it sure seemed like I had racially biased tendencies. It wasn't that I didn't know the definition, but I needed to see it to calm my nerves. Seriously, why would you take a whole race of people and stuff them into a monolithic box? It's insane at the worst, and it's totally inaccurate to have a single, blanket opinion about an entire race of people. It was time to reexamine my thoughts about white people, to do a deep dive and really explore why I felt the way I did and when it all started.

MY UGLY TRUTH

I had said thousands of times in the past that I did not trust white people. My friends made the same comments. In fact, in a roundabout way, my grandmother was probably the first person who told me to be wary. I grew up in a small town that was 77 percent white, and we faced a plethora of incidents of bias and racism, small and large. One of them still hurts to this day. For as long as I could remember, many people from my community, including some white people, felt that our school system was racist. We all heard the stories, but I had never dealt with it personally; in fact, I'd always felt rewarded for my efforts. I was the senior class president and I'd worked tirelessly to win almost every basketball MVP or honor you could win except All-State. I'd sprung back from a torn ACL months sooner than expected. My average hadn't dropped very much, my rebounding was still in the double figures, and I alternated within the top two to three scorers of our conference. I was a shoo-in for All-State and couldn't wait to play on a team of the state's elite players.

However, the day the All-State list was announced, my name wasn't on it. I was crushed. One of my teammates made the list, and another received honorable mention. I knew I was at least good enough to make honorable mention! I was happy for my teammates, but I knew I deserved to be there, too. The following Monday at school was awkward. It seemed like my coaches were acting weird, but no one knew anything and just told me to forget about it—I had been overlooked "for some reason."

Months later, I was at Walmart with my dad and ran into a coach from one of our rival schools. He said, "Hey Grant, I was really disappointed that you weren't named to the All-State team. You should have been there."

Disappointment still weighed on me. "Well, I guess I didn't do that well in the tryouts."

"Those tryouts are a formality," he said. "They know who they are going to pick before you guys even get there." He narrowed his eyes when he looked at me. "Either your coaches forgot or just didn't turn in your paperwork."

The knife in my back turned deeper. I was so upset. I felt used by my coaches. I had played for them with a bad ankle, I played with a fever over 100 degrees, I had played with my knee constantly hurting after a torn ACL, and they had done everything in their power to get me ready to play during those times. I thought they really cared about me. But when it came to something that mattered, they had forgotten my paperwork? It didn't make sense. What I should have done was marched into their offices and demand to know what happened and at least hear their side of the story, but I didn't. I felt like they had intentionally not turned in my paperwork.

Slowly, reality dawned on me. My coaches were white, my teammates whose paperwork they did not forget to turn in were white, and in my teenage mind, this was a race issue. Why did they forget my paperwork? They only cared about them and now it was time for me to look out for us. The worst part is this—one of the girls who made the All-State team had been one of my closest friends since the fifth grade. The episode drew a proverbial line on the court. Our fathers got into an argument about it, and their relationship was never the same. Hurtful things were said on both sides, but I think my dad gave the worst verbal lashing. As a result, I began to deal with them differently.

For most of us, bias has been an unrecognizable part of our upbringing. It has been unconscious.

From that day onward, I felt with every inch of my soul that these things only happened because I was black. Maybe it wasn't so, but because no one ever explained it to me, I'd gone my entire life pissed off about it. Outside of myself, I thought about similar disappointments that had befallen my friends and family. They all seemed to reflect racism. I also thought about the white people whom I absolutely loved and considered family. I trusted them, but I was cautious.

Nope, I wasn't racist, but I recognized that I had a definite bias. It affected me personally and professionally. It needed to be fixed, and quickly.

UNCONSCIOUS BIAS

The silver lining was that I finally understood why my clients didn't get it. These thoughts are deeply rooted. For most of us, bias has been an unrecognizable part of our upbringing. It has been unconscious. The ones feeding it to us probably didn't recognize it themselves, and they may have even encouraged these attitudes as a way to protect us from the type of experiences they faced in their own lives.

It's hard to get rid of a lesson you learned before you could form your own thoughts and opinions—especially if the lesson came to you from the people you trust most in the world. That is how each of us carries biases into adulthood, often unknowingly.

According to Dictionary.com, bias is a *"particular tendency, trend, inclination, feeling, or opinion, especially one that is preconceived or unreasoned."* Another definition refers to *"unreasonably hostile feelings or opinions about a social group; prejudice."*

Translation: You don't like or you are hostile toward others based purely on your unfounded opinions of them. Hmmm, something is missing.

This definition does not fit my bias. I have what I call validated bias. I know it sounds like a fancy way of dressing up an excuse, but indulge me for a moment.

Validated bias is closely related to subjective validation, "*a cognitive bias by which a person will consider a statement or another piece of information to be correct if it has any personal meaning or significance for them.*"[2] **Validated bias is my own term. It is different from prejudice because it is based upon actual experiences that have negatively influenced your way of thinking.** For example, my firm performed in-depth interviews for a Fortune 500 energy company. We interviewed over 300 of their employees to understand how they felt about D&I in their company. One of the interviewees explained that she had been with the company for twenty-five years and had been patiently working and waiting for her supervisor to retire so she could take her position. She filled in for this supervisor when she was sick or on vacation. When the time came for her supervisor to retire, she was told that she was not qualified for the position because she did not have a degree. The company would be filling the position with an external person who had just graduated from college, and to add insult to injury, she had to train the youngster for the job she felt she had rightfully earned. She shared with me that the experience caused her to feel "a certain way" toward young people. She understood that this was not the young woman's fault, but she admitted that she had a real problem training her, and even disliked seeing and interacting with other young professionals in the company. She constantly heard the company executives refer to the new college grads as the company's future leaders. In tears, she asked, "Where does this leave me? I have been here working hard. I'm not a young professional, but I'm not so old that I'm ready to retire. I still want to grow and move

---

2 http://www.psychologyconcepts.com/subjective-validation/ (accessed: Jan. 15, 2017)

up in this company."

Her bias toward young people was validated by her experiences of losing her promotion to one and hearing executives praise them as the future of the company. These messages told her she had no place at the company unless she was fine with being stagnant. Validated bias does not mean you are right or justified. It simply means that a personal experience affected you so much that it has changed the way you feel toward a certain group or subset of people. It's also more difficult to let it go because you have "evidence" for your feelings.

Our biases play a huge part in how we live our daily lives, whether we own up to it or not.

The reason I have a bias and I'm not racist is that I don't feel that my race is superior to any other race. I love my race, but I don't think that people of other races should be treated unequally. However, I do have a belief that white people may treat me differently, may not have my back, or may not regard me as equal to my peers of another race.

Many people don't understand and most don't give a damn that many of our feelings are rooted in old biases. In fact, if you asked a room of people to raise their hand if they have a bias toward another person, I can guarantee from my experience in training employees that over 70 percent of the people in the room will not raise their hand. It's not just because some are embarrassed to admit it. Bias does not have top-of-mind awareness. Typically, we don't label our thoughts about others as biases because we have validated these thoughts. In other words, we have a damn good reason for our feelings. Calling yourself "biased" is like owning up to being racist, sexist, classist, homophobic, or xenophobic. We are uncomfortable admitting these shortcomings.

CALLING BS ON BIAS

Our biases play a huge part in how we live our daily lives, whether we own up to it or not. They stunt our personal and professional growth. In undertaking any diversity and inclusion programs or strategies, you have to start with understanding the bias within your organization or team. If you do not assess the bias in your organization and work to understand your employees' baggage, you will face low productivity, stagnant innovation, and lawsuits. I guarantee you that the baggage exists, even if they don't talk about it at work. Employees want to get more education; they deal with sick relatives; they have marital struggles or difficulties with racism in their kids' school. Today's ideal employer understands this and wants to know about it.

I admit that I struggled to absorb this wisdom. As a Gen X'er, I functioned under the assumption that no one really cared about your baggage and what you had going on outside of work. If you were blessed enough to have a career, you went to work, performed the duties you were being paid to perform, and then went home and dealt with your personal issues. I've had to accept that the world has changed: to remain competitive in today's workforce, companies have to feed the whole person. If you work in the human resources department, or you are a hiring manager or a supervisor, you will have to accept this new reality, as well. Yes, that means giving a damn about employees' lives outside of work, no matter what that lifestyle or identity looks like.

When you are talking about a subject like bias, the first step is to understand yourself and your belief system. What you put into the universe is what you get back from the universe. You first have to understand that it's all BS When you place an entire group of people into a negative space in your mind, whether it's because they are white, gay, female, transgender, or whatever, and even if you have a damn good reason for doing so… It is BS-ish, right? I can call BS on my bias and I hope by the time you are finished reading this chapter, that you can call it on yours, as well.

BS EQUALS BIAS SYNAPSE

Am I talking about bullshit? Look, I'm from cattle country, but we're not going there. Actually, here, BS stands for bias synapse. I coined this term as a play on words to help loosen up the tough subject matter. It works. As I have evolved, so has my term. It is now predicated upon research from author and renowned professor and brain researcher at New York University, Joseph LeDoux. In his words, "You are your synapses. They are who you are." Thanks to LeDoux's research and theories, I can add scientific heft to bias synapse and explain the brain's role in our biased feelings. Think back to eighth-grade science for a moment. A synapse in its most basic form is how the brain communicates between brain cells. LeDoux takes this a step further and says, "Synapses are the channels through which we think, act, imagine, feel and remember." He goes on to say, "Synapses are the junctions (spaces) between neurons, which encode and store information, which is accessible to us through memory." He feels that the synapses that occur in your brain are literally what make you you. Memory is the synaptic result of learning, and it plays a major role in gluing your personality together. Not everyone fully agrees with LeDoux's work, but all neuroscientists agree that the synapse is where communication between brain cells occurs. Interesting stuff, right? If all these important things truly occur in the synapse, so does bias. Experiences, thoughts, and memories create your life. These happen across the synapse. We don't come

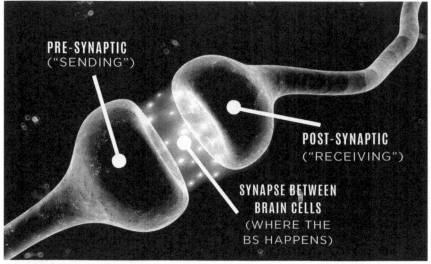

PRE-SYNAPTIC
("SENDING")

POST-SYNAPTIC
("RECEIVING")

SYNAPSE BETWEEN
BRAIN CELLS
(WHERE THE
BS HAPPENS)

SYNAPSIS BETWEEN NEURONS

into the world with biases; we have all seen pictures of babies of different races playing together and hugging and kissing each other. Biases develop from fear—so why are we so scared of each other? We are taught to be afraid, and we have learned it so smoothly that we don't even recognize it in ourselves. Once something or someone hurts you, whether the act is intentional or not, your brain encodes the danger and alerts you so you don't experience that pain again. Think about it: you are on an elevator. It stops at the next floor. A man gets on the elevator who makes you uncomfortable. He is wearing a black trench coat and it's ninety degrees outside.

He is unkempt and staring at you intently. You exit the elevator in the parking garage. So does he. As you are walking to your car, he grabs you. After experiencing this incident, every time you see someone in a long, black trench coat, you immediately feel anxiety. Your body tenses up. Your brain reminds you of what happened last time; you are alert and avoid the situation. This is healthy. You need to remember, protect yourself, and get out of harm's way, right? However, the brain will act on autopilot until you give it more information. Every person in a black trench coat is not out to attack you. Your bias will become unhealthy if you never make a distinction between your one-time assailant and everyone in the world

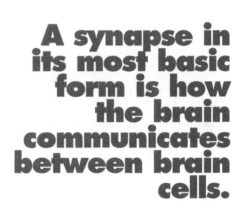

A synapse in its most basic form is how the brain communicates between brain cells.

who owns a similar coat, and if you treat all those other people poorly. Now that we have a clear understanding of bias, let's explore its role in creating the us vs. them paradigm.

PERMISSION: GRANTED TO

- Stay conscious about unconscious bias. Do the work to figure out your bias and give it the top-of-mind awareness it deserves.

- Be real with yourself. Remember your validated bias is not fact. It's based upon actual experiences that negatively influenced your way of thinking.

- Never forget that bias is developed from fear. Conquer your fear.

CHAPTER 3

I WANTED TO BE A MAID

Most of us grew up with an us vs. them mentality. My earliest memory of us vs. them started before I entered kindergarten.

Grandma taught me almost everything I was supposed to learn in school before I showed up on the first day. I had to learn my alphabet, colors, how to count numbers and money, and read a few words. My grandmother was convinced that my future was on the line—already, at age four! When I asked her why I had to learn everything first at her home then again at school, she replied, "Because they may not teach you the way they teach the other chillen'." She said it was important that I knew more, dressed better, and spoke correctly to them. Of course, at that young age, I didn't truly understand what Grandma was saying. I also didn't know who they were so I was confused and upset about these people who were out to rob me of playtime. I already didn't like them and they didn't

What she probably didn't realize is that she inexplicably taught me that there is a them and an us.

have a name or a face.

My grandmother was a maid for a white family in the small town where we lived. Her boss owned a popular department store downtown, so they were considered a good family to work for. My grandmother would take me with her sometimes—if I got sick at school or when her boss's grandkids were in town, she would bring me along to play with them. I loved my grandma so much. I saw how much pride she took in her duties, and I decided that when I grew up, I wanted to be a maid like her.

The last day I would ever play with the other kids went something like this. The adults were sitting on the furniture talking while we played on the floor. My grandmother was working in the kitchen. One of the adults asked us what we wanted to be when we grew up. I don't remember the other kids' responses, but I opened my mouth and announced, aloud in a room full of white people, that I wanted to be a maid like my grandma. The adults began clapping and encouraging my choice. I was smiling, thinking I had made a good choice and that my grandmother would be proud of me, when she flew out of the kitchen.

She got on her knees and grabbed me by both shoulders. Her

glare felt like it was burning a hole straight through to my soul. It caught me off guard, so I held her glare out of fear and curiosity, even though I wanted to look away.

"You will never be a maid!" she said. "Do you think I am doing this because I want to? I'm doing this because I have to. You—you will go to college, become a teacher, or get a job working for the government." (I later learned that a government job meant lifelong stability.)

Thinking back, it seemed like everything in the room was on pause. There was complete silence and a weird feeling that I now know as awkward or unease among the adults. I didn't even know what college was, but I knew by the look in Grandma's eyes that I was going.

On our way home that day, my grandmother explained that she always wanted to be a nurse. She said, during those days, that there were only a few places where a black woman could be a nurse. One of those places was Chicago. She had an aunt who lived there, but her mother hadn't allowed her to go, so instead she joined a local nurses' auxiliary and ended up working as an underpaid maid for the majority of her life until her boss died.

I wondered if my grandmother was furious because I'd played into the white family's expectations of me or that someone had failed to help me understand that I could do so much more. Looking back, I think even her anger was steeped in fear. She wanted a better life for my sister and me than she had created for herself. Of course, at such a young age, I didn't understand this. I just thought she would be proud of me because I wanted to be like her. Ola Mae Knox was not your typical old school black grandma—she was not a tough disciplinarian. There were certain things we knew she didn't play about, though. One was her religion. She honored her Christianity like gang members honor their colors. And over the years, we were all about to learn that she also didn't play about education. Every birthday card she gave us from little children to adulthood included a poem about education.

"Listen my child before you grow old; a good education is greater than gold. Silver and gold will vanish away; but a good education will never decay."

My grandmother changed the trajectory of my life that day. She demanded that I earn a better life for myself. And, I had the option to do it anywhere I wanted—not just in Chicago. What she probably didn't realize is that she inexplicably taught me that there is a them and an us. My young mind understood that there were different rules and that they made them up. It also felt like these people were the enemy, but I still didn't quite understand who they were.

I finally found out who they were on a trip to the store with my grandma. As we were getting out of the car, she demanded I tuck in my shirttail (as she called it). I was not happy about it because my shirt wasn't supposed to be tucked in. It wasn't the style of the short-set. Grandma did not care. She said I would have to stay in the car if I didn't tuck in my shirt. The threat of being left alone in the car released the floodgate of tears from my eyes. Normally, this would have worked, but nope, Grandma still didn't care. She bent down and started shoving my shirt into my shorts.

"Stop all that devilish crying! These people gone think you ain't been raised right!"

She got my shirt tucked it and took off striding toward the store. "Who, Grandma?" I asked as I raced to catch up with her. She turned toward me with a frustrated look and said, "White folks, chile."

Oh my God! I finally knew who they were. They were everywhere and it seemed like they were really going to be a pain in my ass. It is important to be clear: my grandmother never said anything outright negative about white people. She simply felt, based on her very real

This world is not equal, but that doesn't mean those who are different can't make a difference.

experiences, that we may not be treated the same as our Caucasian peers. Looking back, she made it her business to make sure that we knew the things we needed to know so that we would be able to compete in this world. She may not have always known how to teach us what she felt we needed to know, but she made sure we knew how to recognize the situations when we needed to be different because they would notice.

US VERSUS THEM

These stories make a case for how easily bias is interjected into our lives. The person who taught me to be biased was only trying to protect me. She wanted to make sure I got a fair start in life. Everyone who encountered my grandmother knew her love of people and God. Nevertheless, when someone you love is constantly teaching you an unspoken and even sometimes spoken lesson in your formative years, you don't understand the long-term effects. As you grow, your own experiences reinforce your bias, you realize that because there is an us vs. them, you need to look out for the group in which you belong.

I lived in an overwhelmingly Caucasian city that was three percent African American. The neighborhood I lived in was predominately black. In fact, I would venture to say that most of the black people who lived in Sapulpa, Oklahoma during those years lived in my neighborhood. But was I thinking about that as a child? Of course not. I simply thought it was an awesome place to grow up.

In my childhood neighborhood, people seemed to care about

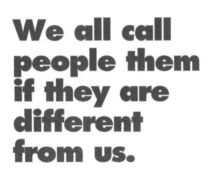
We all call people them if they are different from us.

each other. My grandparents lived a few streets over, and so did four of my aunts and all my cousins and friends. I would go to the neighborhood gym and play basketball almost every day, and I knew my older cousins would always be there to watch out for me. My grandfather was the pastor of a tiny church that I attended all day on Sunday and every other night that it was open.

In seventh grade, my mother decided that we needed a different environment. We left everything we knew and moved across town to an all-white neighborhood. This neighborhood was boring. No basketball courts and no one hanging out. When I walked out my door in the old neighborhood, there were kids riding bikes and someone was usually barbecuing.

There might even be music playing or a card or domino game going on in someone's back yard. Comparatively, this new place looked dead. It seemed people only came outside to walk to their cars or water their grass. If that wasn't bad enough, someone set our trashcan on fire a week or so after we moved in, and one of our neighbors came over to politely tell my dad to keep his kids out of their yard because, even though he didn't mind, his wife didn't care for black people. Our neighbors across the street had kids the same age as my sister and me, but they would call us niggers and run in the house before we could catch them.

We hated living there! It became a daily ambition, finding a way to somehow get "across town" every day to our old safe, fun, black neighborhood. It seemed like my mom was the only one who liked this new place. She was now in college and taking voice and diction classes, which also made life in the house unbearable at times. She was correcting everything we said so we sounded what we called "white." It drove me crazy. We could no longer say, "I'm fina go to the store." It was now, "I'm getting ready to go to the store," or, "I'm going to the store." No more sentences that began with "You be," or "She be." Instead, it was now, "You are," or "She is." We had to enunciate. Doe became door and stoe became store.

I now understand that the voice and diction lessons were one of the best things she could have done for us. It was also very courageous and brave. I don't think many people understood her thinking, and she probably didn't have many people she could share her thoughts with during that time. Admittedly, it seemed like she was removing everything that was familiar and fun in order to move to white suburbia—a place where no one wanted us and we had to act like them. Black kids grow up in a different world, no matter where they come from. We grow up with a resilience instilled in us as children. We are raised to understand that life will be different, even unfair, and the road will not be easy. Life is not easy for anyone, but it seems even harder for us. We are raised to believe that whatever we endeavor to do, we have to do it a hundred times better than anyone else does or we will not even be considered for the job. We feel that we have to dress better and know more, just to level the playing field. Even then, sometimes we are still not on equal footing.

Us vs. them crosses over into the business realm daily. I am meticulous about every piece of communication that leaves my office. E-mail messages, presentations, mailings...there can be no mistakes, and it causes a lot of anxiety if I notice mistakes later. Whenever we are required to offer a proposal to a potential client, we always go above and beyond what is needed. When I merged with the white-owned PR firm and saw their proposals, I was in awe of how little information they included. Hell, I was jealous. I continually saw them submit two or three pages while we pored over ten to fifteen. My peers told me many times that they couldn't believe how much we typically included. Clients said that they didn't usually receive proposals as thorough as ours. It made me feel proud, but I'd learned that going above and beyond was also a necessity.

THE WORLD IS NOT EQUAL

I truly believe that we have to make our way no matter what our circumstances are. This world is not equal, but that doesn't mean those who are different can't make a difference. The truth is that because of the way most black kids grow up, we carry a huge distrust of white people, or we secretly admire their lives because it seems that the world of privilege is placed at their feet. I grew up with a lot of love from many people. Not only did my family push me to believe that I could be whatever I wanted to be in this world, but I also had a whole community pulling for me—or at least that is how I felt.

Diversity does not create the us-versus-them dynamic. People and their biases do. We label people who are not like us them. Because they don't fall into our culture, ethnicity, race, gender, age, sexuality, or religion, we see them as a group apart from who we are. We all call people them if they are different from us.

The us group contains the people we all think we fit in with. And we probably do belong—as long as this group contains only those who look, act, and think as we do. We all want to be a part of this group. We think it's where we belong, and to most of us, it's familiar. Us brings a feeling of comfort and kinship.

No matter who you are, however, your group membership changes depending upon who you ask. To some, you fall in the us category. To others, you fall into the them category. Can you see why this mentality makes no sense? We each embody a set of great, unique differences. I hope we can one day identify as one people working to make this world one where we all fit in. Even so, I would wager that most D&I practitioners would be happy for our world to change to work themselves out of a job. In the meantime, we all need diversity and inclusion training.

HUMANKIND IS INTERCONNECTED

Us vs. them seems to be how most people view diversity and inclusion. Because of this mentality, the concept seems adversarial. We begin to think, if we include them, what happens to us? Will they take our jobs? How will my neighborhood look or change if they move in?

What turns many people off from embracing the concepts of diversity and inclusion, especially in the workplace, is that it feels like they are being forced to hire them, promote them and spend thousands on diversity programs to make them feel comfortable. At the core of us vs. them, it seems that you are being forced to "like" people you don't understand. If not, you risk being sued, fired, or alienated as a pariah in your office.

An associate from a large company shared a situation about an employee who didn't wear deodorant. This man was from another country and apparently, his culture didn't embrace the American habit of wearing deodorant. The office had daily complaints about his body odor. Other than his hygiene, he was a great employee and everyone liked him. No one wanted to offend him by asking him to use deodorant, so they thought leaving an anonymous note on his desk was the best course of action. Can you imagine how alienated this guy probably already felt? He was the only person of his race and culture in a room full of people who couldn't stand his smell.

To people from other countries, Americans also carry a smell that is displeasing to others. In fact, many of our hygiene practices are cultural imports from other countries. In situations like this, you have to remember humanity. One man should not stand alone on an island surrounded by sharks ready to eat him alive. Incidents like this are an opportunity for you to be inclusive. My solution to this enigma would have been to have an honest and respectful conversation with the employee. The human resources department has to have these kinds of conversations a lot. This would have been no different. If your company has a diversity and inclusion director, they may be better prepared to facilitate the conversation. People appreciate honesty even if it stings a little.

The fact is, for most people, this is the same struggle we're all facing every day in our own way. We are all diverse, even in the ways that aren't the big social issues of the day. It is important to know that humankind is interconnected and that D&I is the best way to expose that truth. Diversity isn't about us vs. them, but about how our interconnectedness plays a part in a better quality of life for all of us.

There is no them. It is only us.

All of us—one nation supposedly indivisible. If we don't figure out how to be one functioning body, we will suffer the consequences, as have so many before us. We must each figure out in our own way that what affects one of us will eventually affect all of us.

PERMISSION: GRANTED TO

- Be responsible for the example you set. Realize that what you teach others, whether intentional or unintentional, may have long-term effects. Be conscious of how it may shape who that person becomes.

- Fight for unity. Diversity does not create the us vs. them dynamic. People and their bias do. Strive to identify as one people working to make the world a place where we all fit in. Show the world humankind is interconnected and that there is no them, only us.

CHAPTER 4
THE PERMISSION: GRANTED CONCEPT

Our personal biases permeate our behavior toward one another.

As an executive, you may be thinking, "Who cares about personal issues? Employees need to come and do the job that I hired them to do." That's a great question, and I agree with the principle. Reality, however, shows us that is an unrealistic and unrewarding approach to the workplace. Unfortunately, our internal biases don't patiently wait outside the office door. Unless we make a conscious effort to do otherwise, we bombard our colleagues' lives with our issues eight hours a day, which can slow productivity and kill innovation. In my experience, the only thing that works to counteract this drain is to put emphasis on the well-being of the total person.

The Permission: Granted tool is simple and powerful, and like anything that is both simple and powerful, it cuts deep. It requires your honesty. It requires commitment. It might even require a little discomfort. And here is why. I have read more diversity

You are the problem.

and inclusion books than I can count. Most of these books focus on analytical information, measurements, and complex diversity concepts. However, here is the simple truth: the topic of discussion that matters most is YOU! Most issues that deal with diversity and inclusion begin with the people that unconsciously commit offenses toward others. I know that may be hard to hear. Now is not the time for a thin skin. We need hard truths. As I said before, companies don't have diversity problems. They have people problems!

You are the problem. Stop and let that sink in for a moment. What does it cost you to play along with this thought experiment for a minute? The worst that can happen is that you disagree with me. The best that can happen is that you decide that my two decades of experience might be on to something, and you go off, design, and implement an organization-wide initiative that transforms your group's productivity and energy, all the while avoiding that lawsuit that is lurking in the shadows. It is imperative that you provide an outlet for everyone in your organization. Not only will some of the people be more likely to feel included, but also you will connect with others whose experiences have caused them to carry a validated bias, and thus feel differently about their diverse coworkers. Their behavior could end up costing your company millions.

The concept of Permission: Granted is that it gives people permission to feel how they need to feel about issues that surround diversity, inclusion, and most importantly, bias. We often feel vilified for our beliefs and thoughts, so we keep these feelings bottled up inside. Those feelings will eventually surface. It may be as a single explosion, or as a steady simmering of small issues that can mean the end of friendships or even a marriage. Of all places, I saw the perfect example of this dynamic on television, watching Divorce Court. (I know I may have just lost some IQ points in your mind, but I can't help it; I really like the show.) Anyway, this particular case involved an interracial couple who met in college. The woman was African American and the man was Caucasian. They had been in love since their freshman year. They were taunted relentlessly by both races about their relationship, but one night, the taunting turned violent. The man had to have reconstructive surgery because the assailants broke his face when they pistol-whipped him.

As he dealt with his physical and emotional wounds, his fiancée didn't give him the support he needed. She told him that she was very sorry that it happened but that they would have to rise above it together; they went on to get married, but the issue simmered between them until it drove them to divorce court. The judge handled this situation perfectly by having an honest conversation with the man. She asked him if his real problem was that since black men had beaten him that he now had an issue with all black men. He replied, "Yes, I think you're right." As far as his wife was concerned, he felt that she should not trust black men, either. Worse, his love for her became more complicated because she was black. The judge then asked him if he would feel the same way toward all white men if they had been the aggressors. The man answered, "Probably not."

I thought this was brilliant because it drives home the concept behind my Three-Step Process, which is to *Identify, Own, and Confront Your BS* I thought it was fair that the man felt the way he felt and he deserved to wallow in it for a while. Honestly, I might have felt similarly. Who wouldn't? Yet he didn't feel permitted to verbalize his feelings, and he felt guilty for feeling them in the first place, so he just kept it inside until it eroded his relationship with his wife.

The moral is this—we have to let people feel how they feel and make them comfortable enough to verbalize their difficulty so they can work through it. Change begins with honesty.

PERMISSION: GRANTED TO HAVE QUESTIONS

Many of us have questions about diverse groups. We want to know more about racial groups, people with disabilities, or people in the LGBTQ community. Most of us don't have an opening to ask questions without giving offense.

Some years ago, I hired a man to work on my sales team. He used a wheelchair. I was nervous about all kinds of things, especially how to accommodate his needs in the office. Admittedly, I was even worried that I could be sued if I didn't have certain things in place.

One day, he and I needed to ride to an appointment together. My SUV was difficult for him to enter, so it made more sense for him to drive us. His car's brakes were located on the steering wheel; he completely operated the vehicle with his hands. I won't lie—I was nervous. He obviously sensed my fear, and in response, he started weaving in and out of traffic. I kept trying to hold a conversation but I was secretly pushing a nonexistent brake on my side. He began to drive faster. When I finally couldn't take it anymore, I gasped, "Pull this damn car over." He burst out laughing and said, "You need to relax. I know how to drive."

I immediately calmed down, and he returned to the speed limit. After forcing me to breach the silence around our physical differences, we had the best relationship from that day forward. I was able to ask him many questions about his disability, and he had the best attitude; he also loved being able to cut in line because he was in a wheelchair. He'd lightly run into people with his chair. They would profusely apologize and then let him in the front of the line. He was humorous and ornery. I began to see his personality and not his wheelchair. Giving yourself permission to see the humanity in others will break down hesitancy and cautiousness.

Why was I uncomfortable in the first place? Because he was different. He didn't walk on his legs. It sounds like BS even as I write these words. If I had dwelled on this one difference any longer, I would have alienated an incredible employee and missed an important friendship. At first, I put so much energy into my fear of saying the wrong thing. I wanted to be able to accommodate his needs. Most important, I made assumptions about what he could and could not do. In this case, it wasn't as much bias as it was a true case of bullshit. If I had given myself permission to ask him the questions I needed and wanted to ask in a respectful way, he would have never tried to kill me in traffic just to show me how stupid I was being. It should not have been his job to make me feel comfortable, but I will be forever grateful that he did. When we don't take the time to understand a perspective or lifestyle different from our own, we are stuck in a pissy-polite state that makes others uncomfortable. **Pissy-polite is my term for any behavior exuded by a person who feels obligated to be polite but can't successfully fake a warm interaction.**

We have to let people feel how they feel and make them comfortable enough to verbalize their difficulty so they can work through it.

Alternatively, it can be a seemingly polite action accompanied by a subtle, sarcastic undertone that conveys disdain or dislike.

Others can feel your vibe, even if you avoid them just so you don't give offense. If you do have to be around them, you make sure to keep it short and to the point. Your personality comes off as cold and unaccepting, which translates as a lack of interest in their presence, let alone their lives.

Can you imagine what this does to a group of people who are charged with working together to innovate your next product? What about a team that needs to come up with a new platform for your online company? They can't get past their own discomfort and BS to provide you with the best they have to offer. Instead, you get a mediocre product or service that has minimal success on the market.

Permission: Granted has been a personal journey for me. Through my three-step process, I gave myself permission to feel what I needed to so I could be free in my personal life and productive in my professional life. You can do the same. In the next three chapters, I will walk you through each step using real life anecdotes and my clients' experiences. Once you put the work into these steps, you will be able to move through your feelings. It will also be a work in progress because every negative experience will bring back the bad feelings, but if you want to, you can change it.

PERMISSION: GRANTED TO

- Be accountable. Our personal biases permeate our behavior toward others. It's not them, it really is you.

- Be committed to the process. Being honest may make you uncomfortable. That's normal—fight through it. Work through your bias, no matter how you feel. The goal is worth it.

- Be on the lookout for pissy-polite people. Understand these people are a detriment to your workplace environment.

CHAPTER 5
STEP ONE
PERMISSION:GRANTED TO IDENTIFY YOUR BS

The first step in the Permission: Granted process is to Identify Your BS.

This step is important because most people don't realize that they have BS—a bias synapse. Understanding that I had a validated bias against white people floored me. For one, I am Ms. Ambassador for Diversity. In addition, I have many white people in my life whom I truly love. For me, figuring out my bias would help me professionally—to sell my services better and further help my clients understand how removing these barriers leads to a competitive advantage.

Personally, we all owe it to the world to leave it a better place than we found it—to work at not perpetuating our biases so that the generations after us don't have to keep discussing the same issues. After I discovered that I held a bias, I began to wonder what other biases I mistook for truths. Where else in my life was I being unfair to others, transmitting bias, and possibly losing out on awesome new friends? To help me—

and my clients—in this difficult self-scan, I developed the BS Finder. It helps indicate whether we have bias and where we may have gotten it.

THE BS FINDER

This tool is a simple, guided thought process. It includes the following:

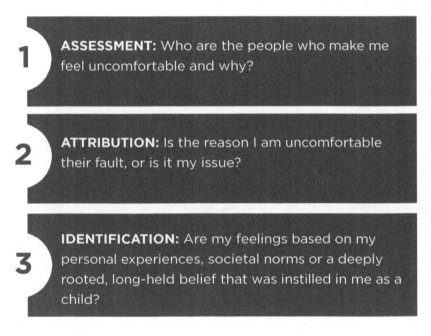

1 **ASSESSMENT:** Who are the people who make me feel uncomfortable and why?

2 **ATTRIBUTION:** Is the reason I am uncomfortable their fault, or is it my issue?

3 **IDENTIFICATION:** Are my feelings based on my personal experiences, societal norms or a deeply rooted, long-held belief that was instilled in me as a child?

Here is what I identified as my BS. As I searched for other biases, I realized that I didn't understand girls who want to be boys and boys who want be girls—i.e., the transgender person.

Allow me to walk you through my thought process as I identified whether or not I truly had a bias. You will apply this process to yourself or your team, as well.

ASSESSMENT

This step is quick. I assessed my level of comfort and realized that in being around a transgender person, I experienced a level of unease. Why? This made little sense to me—I have always been able to

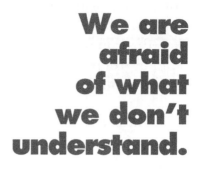
We are afraid of what we don't understand.

find common ground with others. I also don't believe that it is necessary to completely understand and agree with every aspect of a person's life in order to be friends. Yet in being honest with myself, transgender people made me uneasy.

ATTRIBUTION

In this step, be careful about understanding your discomfort. Sometimes we are uneasy with a person because of their personality traits—sometimes it has nothing to do with bias. Someone who is abrasive, touchy, confrontational, or accusatory might set you off. For instance, people who invade my personal space when talking to me make me uncomfortable. I don't need our noses touching in order to have a conversation! It makes me want to avoid close talkers because no matter how much I back up, they keep bringing it in.

The bottom line is this: we may not like everything about another person, but that does not constitute a bias, either. Not liking someone because of their skin color, who they choose to sleep with, or their gender expression, or if certain types of people just don't fit into the box you would like them to stay in and that makes you uncomfortable, it's starting to look a whole lot like bias.

My discomfort with transpeople was clearly my issue. No one from the LGBTQ community had ever done anything to me. In fact, this community has been one of the most loving and accepting groups I've encountered. I finally realized that I truly did not understand the transgender world.

On the surface, I was uncomfortable because I wasn't sure how to address some of them. Pronouns are extremely important. Many times, I truly cannot tell where a transgender person is in the process of transition, and the last thing I ever want to do is give offense by tripping over a pronoun. So, I found conversations awkward because I was focused on avoiding saying anything offensive. Further, on the deepest level, I couldn't understand why someone would want to put his or her body and family through such an extreme process.

Most troubling to me, though, was why my lack of understanding someone else's gender expression caused me to be a standoffish, pissy-polite person. Where did this come from?

IDENTIFICATION

We buy into our own bullshit whenever it suits us.

Whenever someone falls outside of a societal norm, they are bound to step on toes. On some level, we are afraid of what we don't understand. Transgender people are not a societal norm, although that continues to change more every day. We are not used to seeing men living as women or women living as men. We might feel fine watching a documentary about gender expression, or feel comfortable ignoring a person's gender dysphoria as long as they are hiding it at home, but we lose our minds when a transwoman is bold enough to leave the house wearing a bra. It's as if we think, "How dare they walk out of their closet and into street where I have to be inconvenienced by looking at someone who chooses to wear the clothes they bought with their own money! Who gave them permission to live their lives on their terms?"

TOTAL BS!

I have never really given a damn what society considers normal, because to me, normal is boring. Therefore, I began to recognize my issue with transpeople as a deeply rooted belief. Most of my family and the community I grew up in all believed that anyone from the LGBTQ community is going straight to hell. As a bisexual woman who has been in a loving relationship with a female partner for ten years, I went through hell on earth – forget the one that they were concerned about - examining my belief system, especially as it related to my family and community. My family has been supportive, although I have no doubt that some of them are still praying for my salvation. A long time ago, I came to a simple understanding for myself: "The same God that made you, made me. This same God loves me. This same God knows my heart. This same God blessed me to meet this woman and knew that I would be in this relationship. For this same God to set me up to burn in a fiery pit for the rest of my life is not the love of God." I'm sure there are many theologians and religious people who would love to debate my simple theory, but that is not my point here. Even though I had gone through this entire process for myself, I still struggled to apply it to others. My church upbringing had also taught me that God didn't make mistakes. In other words, if God made you male, you were supposed to be male. We buy into our own bullshit whenever it suits us.

When you really think about what life must be like for a transgender person, it is hard to believe that someone would undertake the mental anguish, physical pain, emotional turmoil, and even financial ruin if gender dysphoria were simply a feeling they could control. I cannot imagine going through life constantly at odds with my biological body.

Deep down, I was having trouble with this issue because according to all that I had been taught, I really was going to hell—and so was everyone else living this abomination. It was incredibly hard to deal with my BS because I also had to figure out how to deal with everyone else's while leaving my family and friendships intact. It is a lot more difficult to get rid of your BS when it is deeply rooted. Ultimately, however, it's important to know where your BS originates so you can appreciate how difficult some biases are to overcome. It's a process. It requires thorough examination and consistent work.

In order to help you, I have identified four factors that reinforce deep-rooted bias: personal experience, family, friends, and media.

PERSONAL EXPERIENCE

Negative personal interactions with someone often contributes to bias. For instance, I mentioned a woman earlier who formed a bias against millennials because she had to train a millennial to perform a job that she felt was rightfully hers. She felt threatened, taken advantage of, misunderstood, and abandoned. This experience caused her to form a bias against millennials and young professionals, in general.

FAMILY

When our biases are taught to us as a worldview or strategy for navigating life, we are hazy on whether it's wrong to feel a certain way toward others who are different. We may not realize our bias until someone points it out or we have a negative interaction. Most devastating of all is when we never realize it.

Bias learned through family is usually fear-based, generational, and validated. A perfect example is my grandmother. She was a black woman born in 1923. Her bias was validated and well-meaning but definitely fear-based. She saw the world through a lens that did not treat black people equally. She knew from her own experiences that life would be more difficult for my sister and me than for white girls our age. She pressed education (and God) at every opportunity. As a way to protect me, she taught me not to trust them and to work harder

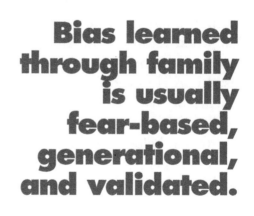

Bias learned through family is usually fear-based, generational, and validated.

to achieve anything. She did not want us to end up as casualties in the never-ending war on race.

The difficulty with family and personal experience is that these biases are more deeply rooted and much harder to overcome because they are often passed on to you by people you love and trust.

FRIENDS

Our friends are like extended family. We trust their product referrals, experiences with doctors, and recommendations for dating, daycares, and recipes. Their word-of-mouth is as golden as our family's. As a good friend, we embrace our friends' positive experiences. We also get pissed on behalf of our friends when they endure a negative experience. We tend to accept our friends' opinions without question, especially as teens and young adults. Unfortunately, we absorb their biases, as well. Bias learned through our friends can come from peer pressure and be fear-based because we don't want to lose our friends.

After working together for many years, one of my Hispanic colleagues has become a good friend. She shared with me that when Latinos immigrate to the U.S., they are told by friends and family to be afraid of black people. This fear-based bias is introduced at an early age. As a result, when arriving in the U.S., one of her biggest fears was of black people. Of course, her interactions with cool black people like myself helped to dispel this fear, but you can imagine how many people still walk around with this bias instilled in them because it came from people they trust.

MEDIA

Media plays a huge role in our lives. With the advent of social media, we are receiving information as it happens from all parts of the world. Whether we realize it or not, it influences our decisions. As we learned in the last election, media does not always depict the truth. People of color have known this for a long time and have always noticed biased reporting and negative stereotyping. They have also always understood how powerful media can be when telling your story. Media teaches us about culture, whether those lessons are true or not.

Growing up in the 1970s and 1980s, I watched a lot of *Leave it to Beaver, I Love Lucy, Good Times,* and *The Jeffersons.* The white shows led me to believe that all white people slept in separate twin beds. The black shows showed married couples in one big bed like my parent's bed. It wasn't until I went to a white friend's house that I realized that her parents also slept in one big bed. I love media—my degree is in journalism and mass communication—but I recognize the inaccuracies in my field. We have to learn media intelligence and seek out our own truths.

Another important antidote is to watch a wide variety of programming. You can learn a lot about the real culture of people of color, about the LGBTQ community, and about different cultures and religions if you seek out a well-rounded understanding of the world. Do not allow your media consumption to reinforce the belief system you already have in place. If you expand your horizons, even beyond your comfort zone, I truly believe media can help you to eradicate some of your long-held biases.

It's time to Identify Your BS. Take some time to think about your biases. Once you are finished with your assessment, write down your attributions and then identify its sources-why you have these biases and where they originated. You will learn a lot about yourself. You may not like all that you learn, but the good news is that my process will move you through it it.

....

....

....

....

....

....

....

....

....

....

....

....

....

....

....

....

....

....

PERMISSION: GRANTED TO

- Proactively examine your surroundings. Look at how you can remove barriers that prevent your organization from having a competitive advantage.

- Get to the bottom of your BS. Use the BS Finder to assess your bias, attribute the source, and identify your feelings.

- Do you! Live life on your terms and allow others to do the same. Understand that you don't have to agree with every aspect of someone's life to accept them.

- Uproot your BS. Remember my four factors that reinforce deep-rooted bias: personal experience, family, friends, and media.

CHAPTER 6
STEP TWO
PERMISSION: GRANTED TO OWN YOUR BS

So far, you probably think, "I'm really glad Risha wrote this book for the straight, white male."

Not true. We all have work to do to be better people. No matter who you are, once you have identified your BS, you have to Own... Your... Shit. Take those feelings that you have been harboring inside yourself and say them aloud. This is important. We keep this stuff in hiding most of the time, but when we say it aloud, it sounds like the BS that it is. This does not have to be a public declaration, but hearing it in your own voice is a crucial step to acknowledging the space that bias takes up in your life.

I said this earlier, but I will keep repeating it: one of the main problems with D&I is that people do not have permission to feel how they need to feel about diversity without guilt, even though that feeling is their truth. Inevitably, people feel forced to hide their feelings, which in turn produces a negative aura. It will continue to spread until they have a positive experience in that area. For instance, you may have adverse feelings regarding someone from the LGBTQ community because your dad realized he was gay after thirty years of marriage to your mom and it tore your family apart. This is real, it is valid, it hurts like hell, and you have permission to feel messed up about it. Say it out loud. Give yourself permission to go there.

FIVE WAYS YOU GIVE BIAS SPACE IN YOUR LIFE

There are several responses to bias. We have only discussed *validated bias* but the others are just as important. As you own your bias, it's important for you to understand the different responses and how they affect you. They are *validation, passivity, shame, acceptance,* and *denial.* Which one of these do you use?

PASSIVITY

Besides validation, the most likely response is to be passive about bias—to ignore it. This can be a subconscious choice, but it's important that we start recognizing the tendency in ourselves. Haven't we all been in a situation where we should have spoken up? Instead, though, we either didn't realize it until it was too late or chose to avoid a confrontation by saying nothing. This is the coward's response.

It's easy to ignore our shortcomings and much harder to own them. Ignoring your own bias or allowing others to be biased around you perpetuates stereotypes and allows BS to run unchecked. It also makes people think that you agree with their point of view, even if you don't.

SHAME

Those of us who know we have a bias might feel ashamed. Although I had validated my bias regarding white people, I was ashamed that I avoided transgender people. I knew better and I needed to take the time to face it, but because transsexual people weren't part of my everyday life, my shame made me drag my feet. Getting past this particular bias took much longer than it needed to.

ACCEPTANCE

Some people flat-out accept their bias and are perfectly fine with it. This is cool if you are biased about your college football team, but it sucks if you are biased toward a group of people who are just trying to live their lives. It's good that you recognize your bias, but what are you going to do about it? If the answer is nothing, why are you even reading this book?

DENIAL

This is the worst response. I meet so many people who tell me they have no bias, and in almost every case, it is just not true. I once asked an employee to name any bias she might have. She told me she had none. So, I asked her questions:

"Is there a certain group that makes you uncomfortable?" She said no. After going back and forth, I said, "I think you have a problem with LGBTQ people."

She protested for a while and then said. "I guess."

I told her she didn't seem to have a problem with me and my partner. She replied that we don't kiss or show affection in front of her. My next question: "So what if we did?"

"I wouldn't want to see that."

"Why?"

"Because, it's gross."

"Because we are two women?"

"Well, I don't want to see my parents kiss, either."

I told her that no one wants to see their parents kiss. It is not the same thing. I asked again, "Why does it make you uncomfortable for people of the same sex to show affection for each other?

"I don't know. I just think it's gross."

My first thought was WOW! I didn't get mad, because she is entitled to her feelings. Her bias certainly didn't please me, but frankly, I felt better that it was out in the open because I had suspicion she'd felt this way for a long time. Furthermore, she has never been disrespectful to my partner or me. We had a very honest conversation and determined that she has a bias toward LGBTQ people. It is not overt, and no one would probably ever know it, but it is there. Yet this employee and I have a great relationship. She fully accepts and respects me as I am. This further accentuates my point that when you get to know people and take the time to understand them, you can see them for who they are instead of the label you or society assigns to them.

NOBODY GETS A PASS

By the way, if you fall into a diverse category yourself, you need to own your shit, too. There is no doubt that we are on the receiving end of a lot of bias and prejudice, but we are not saints. We tend to own a sense of entitlement to our bias. We feel like we should get a pass on our feelings not only because of what has happened in history but also because of all the things we see happening today, from police brutality to bans on Muslims entering the United States. We seem to be ramping up toward a more biased society. Don't allow it to make you shut down and notice the victimization by others but not take ownership for ways in which you are actually a part of the process. The foundation of owning your BS, however, is taking responsibility for you!

The most radical way for us to combat bias and exclusion right now is to start with ourselves: to seek out and acknowledge our personal racism, sexism, homophobia, ableism, or xenophobia - and then work to change. That's how we become a bulwark against divisiveness.

Remember, I said companies don't have diversity problems. They have people problems. If you did not get that promotion you felt you deserved, ask yourself why. Be real. Did you really deserve it, or have you been late for fifteen of the last thirty days? Do you leave right at 5 p.m. every day even when everyone else stays behind to work on the project? If you're thinking about playing the race card, the LGBTQ card, or the gender card, just be damn sure that the hand you are dealing is a fair win. The way you own your BS is to acknowledge the space it occupies in your life. You own it by accepting your authentic self—bruises, warts, bias and all.

Once you take responsibility for your bias, you will notice things like the fact that most diverse people do not want a promotion because of their diversity. They want it because they have earned it. They do not want you to lower your standards to hire them. They want a fair chance to compete for the position. People want a level playing field on which to earn their opportunities and fully utilize their talent.

SIMPLE LESSONS IN D&I

The entire concept of D&I is simple to grasp because it starts and ends with humanity. It is also simple because everything you need to know about it, you should have learned when you were five years old. Yes, it really is that basic. Discrimination lawsuits are what happens when we don't apply what we learned as children. Here they are again, in case we need a refresher on those kindergarten lessons in equal opportunity.

Do not call people names or talk about them behind their backs. We have all heard this one. And I bet executives from Texaco and Coca-Cola wish their employees had remembered this lesson as they paid out $176 million and $192.5 million, respectively, for calling African Americans niggers (and other reprehensible conversations).

Listen when others are speaking, especially if they are your customers. How difficult is this one, really? Burger King sure wishes it had listened to customer complaints when it paid out $19 million because eighty-six of their restaurants were not wheelchair accessible. It could have complied with the American Disabilities Act, but instead it ended up writing a big check, to boot and then having to comply anyway. Not only did they ignore the disabled community, the fast food chain lost customers because people in wheelchairs could not access the stores.

Work and play well with others. Because the boys refused to play fairly with the girls, Wells Fargo paid $32 million in a lawsuit brought on by their female financial advisors. Additionally,

Ignoring your own bias or allowing others to be biased around you perpetuates stereotypes and allows BS to run unchecked.

Walmart has had five gender discrimination suits filed against them, alongside other discrimination suits. The 2011 class-action lawsuit included 1.5 million female plaintiffs, and until the U.S. Supreme Court rejected the suit, it was thought that Walmart would end up paying the largest settlement in U.S. history. Regardless of the outcome, the suit was costly in dollars, damage to reputation and lost talent.

Be nice. Yes, it sounds elementary. How many times did your mom tell you to be nice, not pissy-polite. There is a difference, and people can feel it. If these companies' employees had remembered their childhood lessons and simply been nicer to their consumers and employees, they could have saved millions. Surely, there is a better way to spend hard-earned profits.

The simplest lesson of all is this: *Treat others the way they want to be treated.*

Most of our big companies get why D&I is important. To them, it's not about color, sexuality, gender, disability—it's about profitability. More and more companies are figuring out that the price of inclusion is a lot cheaper than the price of exclusion. The McKinsey Company has examined diversity in the workplace for years.[3] According to their research:

- Companies in the top quartile for racial and ethnic diversity are 35 percent more likely to have financial returns above their respective national industry medians.

- Companies in the top quartile for gender are 15 percent more likely to have financial returns above their respective national industry medians. In the United States, there is a linear relationship between racial and ethnic diversity and better financial performance: for every 10 percent increase in racial and ethnic diversity on the senior-executive team, earnings before interest and taxes (EBIT) rise 0.8 percent.

- Racial and ethnic diversity has a stronger impact on financial performance in the United States than gender diversity, perhaps because earlier efforts to increase women's representation in the top levels of business have already yielded positive results.

I owned my BS by seeking to understand and respect other people's right to live their lives as they see fit. The truth is that when we do not understand, it's because we don't want to. You do not have to be a genius to know that common courtesy and respect are basic customs. It is okay that you do not understand someone's lifestyle. It is okay that you are uncomfortable, but it is not okay to use someone's identity against them or think the worst of them purely because you

3 http://www.mckinsey.com/business-functions/organization/our-insights/why-diversity-matters (accessed: Feb. 20, 2017)

do not understand. You have to be willing to grow and evolve as a person. I intentionally work on this every day.

In the space provided, write about how you can Own Your BS. What have you told yourself to validate your thoughts and feelings about your own identity or someone else's? How can you seek to better understand the people or groups that you have identified as your BS?

....

....

....

....

....

....

....

....

....

....

....

....

....

....

....

....

....

PERMISSION: GRANTED TO

- Evaluate the space your bias takes up in your life. Is it worth it?
- Self-examine your decision making. What is your response to bias? How it is holding you back?
- Check yourself. Do you feel entitled to bias?

CHAPTER 7
STEP THREE
PERMISSION: GRANTED TO CONFRONT YOUR BS

Let's recap. As a first step, you have admitted that you—like everyone else—sometimes struggle with diversity and have identified your biases.

Second, you have owned your feelings by seeking to understand them. Now it's time to overcome them.

This third step is where many of us get stuck because it is uncomfortable, and we have validated our bias synapse. But we cannot stay here. We must confront our biases. And the only thing more powerful than a bias is the strongest emotion of all: love.

Confronting your BS requires the concept of unconditional love—that is, acceptance. Even if this sounds too touchy-feely to you, it doesn't make it any less true. Unless your heart is

We must confront our biases. And the only thing more powerful than a bias is the strongest emotion of all: love.

made of iron, you are a human being. If you are reading this book, you are a human being who is capable of astonishing kindness and new acceptance, and these feats are both rooted in love.

In my own life, I realized that if I did not make changes, my feelings would turn into hate, or I would begin to treat others as if they were worthless and invisible. By now, you are tired of hearing how I did not trust white people. However, when I decided to do the internal work and confront my bias, it occurred to me that I knew some very cool white people. Some of these people are like family. I realized that the white people I had issues with did not justify my putting a whole race of people into a negative category. I assessed my relationships with every person in my life on a case-by-case basis, regardless of their skin color. In being honest with myself, using my reasons for not trusting white people, I sure as hell should not trust many black people, either. I am around more black people and they have had a larger impact on my life than white people, even in the negative realm. I realized that I simply gave them more grace. I forgave easier because they were part of my comfort zone. Yet if I were to apply my biased logic to those black people who had done me wrong, I should not trust any black people at all.

DOING THE WORK

When I say to confront your bias, I mean to get out of your head and into the world. Get to know someone who triggers your biases. When I perform in-depth interviews for my clients, employees often report avoiding certain people or groups either because they don't want to give offense or because a validated bias has caused them to keep their distance.

CEOs, VPs, HR people, you cannot have hateful, indifferent, or fearful people in your organization. I'm telling you point-blank. It is poisonous to your work environment. These are not diversity problems—these are people problems. As employers, you have to get your head out of the sand and realize that your employees may not be working well together because of bias. No company wants to admit that their workplace is sheltering racism, sexism, homophobia, transphobia, ableism, or any other bias—but it happens all the time. Do a survey. Hire someone to perform in-depth interviews or create a space for people to share their concerns and fears without judgment.

Confronting the negativity will allow you to hit sales goals, provide better services, and make better products. People work hard for you when they know you genuinely care as much about their personal wellbeing as you do about the work you hired them to do.

I confronted my BS with transgender people by asking a transgender woman to lunch. We met as board directors for a local organization. She had also attended an event my company hosted, so I thought she might be open to speaking with me. I asked if she would join me for lunch so that I could get to know her. I was honest: I explained that I had a tendency to avoid transgender people at times because I didn't want to use the wrong pronoun and give offense. I also wanted to learn more about her life. She gave me free rein to ask anything and everything. We had an honest conversation. She told me that any transgender person that gets upset over the wrong pronoun is being too sensitive and that the transgender community understands that sometimes people truly don't know. It reminded me of when I was conducting an interview for a client and the employee shared with me that he'd avoided black people for a long time because someone once got offended that he used *black* instead of *African American.* At the time, I'd said the same thing—"Too sensitive." I interchange these terms daily.

The most important thing I learned from this woman was what I already knew: she has dreams, goals, disappointments, and worries, just as I do. She cares about her family and community. She has bills to pay. She is working to live her life on her terms, just as I am. I found that we had more in common than we had differences. Listening to her speak, I respected the courage it took for her to live her life authentically. I will be forever grateful that she allowed me into her space and opened up to me. She could have told me to kick rocks. It was not her responsibility to educate me and make me comfortable, but you will find that people are open. They will talk to you and share with you. We all seek love, understanding, and acceptance.

Change takes effort, but it is simple if you commit yourself to the process. If you can't handle the emotional stuff, here is the simplest advice I can share. Get over it! Stop making your issue someone else's fault. We all have issues, quirks, or some weird habit that gets on other people's nerves. If you don't, you are probably the most boring person on earth. Recognize that even if someone is not the same color, age, gender, religion, or sexuality as you, they deserve the exact same amount of respect and courtesy as people who

Get over it! Stop making your issue someone else's fault.

look and act like you. If you create reasons to dislike these others, hold them to different standards, or refuse to explore your aversion to them, you are biased. You have internal work to do. I challenge you, as an intelligent and capable person, to look at your list of biases and open yourself up to interact with someone from each group. If your issue is age, ask an older or younger person to lunch. If it's race, ask someone of a different race to grab a cup of coffee. Having lunch with a person who navigates life in a wheelchair will open your eyes to challenges that person faces daily. As you get to know these people and feel more comfortable with them, invite them to hang out. It will be an enriching experience for everyone there. Not only that, but diversity brings flavor to any conversation.

BE INTENTIONAL

One of the most important lessons in this book—and in the world of D&I—is to *be intentional.* The commonality in all three steps (Identify Your BS, Own Your BS, and Confront Your BS) is intentionality. To be inclusive, you have to do it on purpose. If I am not being intentional, I will not be inclusive because we are all creatures of habit. I am a black woman who grew up in a black family and—even though I am from Sapulpa, a predominately white city—I lived in an all-black

The work is never over. Just as none of us is bias-free, we all probably have more than one bias. And we may develop future biases. Keep asking questions and stay open to learning.

neighborhood, went to an all-black church, and so on. I spent time around white people, but mainly at school or school-related functions. See how that works? As a result, I have to interrupt my routine patterns in order to include different people in my life. Otherwise, if I am planning a party and making out an invitation list, more than likely, the majority of the invitees will be black people; it's just my comfort zone.

If you are Jewish, you might frequent Jewish schools, markets, neighborhoods, and synagogues. This is not because you are discriminating, but because it is your culture and comfort. If we are not intentional about being inclusive, there is no way we are going to be. To change it, you have to create top-of-mind awareness of other fun people you know and invite them further into your life. I have found it to be a very enriching experience. I have a friend who is an eclectic, black, bisexual, vegetarian, natural-living Buddhist. Try categorizing her!

Another thing to remember about inclusion is that just because people say we should all play nice does not mean we will. You cannot take a group of people from different cultures, races, backgrounds, religions, and whatever else and assume they will all get along. We do not know each other. Half of us do not get along with our families, and we have known them forever. Progress is messy. Truth is messy. Authenticity is messy. It all starts with conversation. It is about seeking understanding and common ground. It is intentional. And its reward is the beautiful realization that most people have the same feelings, thoughts, wants, and needs that you have.

If you allow yourself to confront your BS and find that you still do not like someone after getting to know them, I guarantee you it has more to do with their personality than their general identity. Dumbasses come in all shades, religions, ages, and genders—the same goes for snobs, loudmouths, flakes, backstabbers, braggarts, liars, and all the rest. These aren't permanent flaws, either, but that's a subject for a different shelf in the bookstore's self-help section. And typically, how you treat someone has more to do with you than with them. Own it. One final point: the work is never over. Just as none of us is bias-free, we all probably have more than one bias. And we may develop future biases. Keep asking questions and stay open to learning.

In the space below, list a few different ideas you have to Confront Your Bias.

....

....

....

....

....

....

....

....

....

....

....

....

....

....

....

....

....

....

PERMISSION: GRANTED TO

- Ask yourself, "Could my thinking be wrong about a particular person or group of people?"

- Wonder, "What should I do to find out?"

- Ask, "Who am I willing to get to know better from my list of bias identifiers?"

- Be intentional and connect. For example, set a deadline for inviting that person out for coffee. Stick to it. See what happens.

PART II:
WORKPLACE

CHAPTER 8

BUILDING AN INCLUSIVE CULTURE

People! People! People! They are the key to building an inclusive culture.

To successfully create the seemingly elusive inclusive workplace, all your strategies should focus on people.

The first section of this book discussed bias. In my years of owning a diversity communications and consulting firm, I have learned that bias is the antithesis to inclusion and humanity. Now that you have permission to get rid of your BS, where do we go from there? We turn our focus to building an inclusive culture. This encompasses diverse recruitment and attracting diverse customers. These are cornerstones to economic advancement and sustainability.

Think about it this way. From the CEO to entry-level employees, everyone must understand how diversity and inclusion (D&I) creates a competitive advantage. Changes as small as going from *Merry Christmas* to *Happy Holidays* can alienate your employee base—so to avoid this problem, you need to communicate why changes are necessary. Competitive advantage is what helps the bottom line. It's also the concept that your employees and colleagues are most likely to grasp. If the messaging is not right, you will lose people—both customers and employees.

People! People! People! They are the key to building an inclusive culture.

Next, you need to create a strategic marketing plan for attracting diverse customers. Given the trillions of dollars in disposable income on the table, it is surprising how many companies still don't direct their advertising or marketing toward diverse groups.

Lastly, make sure that D&I initiatives include a plan for recruiting diverse employees and retaining those employees. If you are going to attract diverse customers, you will need diverse employees with whom your new customers can identify. In helping companies get started, I use five basic guiding principles for my clients.

FIVE GUIDING PRINCIPLES

1. Gain a Personal Commitment from the CEO and Other Senior-Level Executives

Without buy-in from leadership, it is difficult to create an open environment, much less a zero-tolerance policy for discrimination. Every employee needs to understand your organization's culture. This communication can come in the form of a letter, a video, or both. It should be sent through the intranet and be easily accessible to all employees. According to Catalyst.org, 50 percent of employees felt a stronger sense of inclusion when they felt personally attached to their company's core values. The question is, does the other half not feel included because the workplace isn't making an effort to be inclusive, or is it more about indifference? Either way, it's definitely worth exploring because a number that large affects your entire business.

2. Include Diversity and Inclusion Language in All Mission, Purpose, and Core Value Statements

When I graduated from college in 1996, the strategy was to send resumes to any company hiring in your field and take any job that you were offered, even if it was in Timbuktu. That has changed. Millennials are actually choosing employers based on company culture and the city's attributes, such as nightlife, growth, transportation, and culture. High on the list of desirable features is diversity and inclusion. According to Deloitte.com, 83 percent of millennials are engaged when they believe an organization fosters an inclusive culture. Your D&I content should be easy to find. Include a specific tab for it on your site's navigation bar. It should not be forced or inaccurate; it needs to be a true reflection of your culture. If it falls short of reality, your employees will make it known—if not privately to you, then through other, more public channels. Your employees are your company ambassadors—if they speak poorly of your culture, people outside of the company will find out soon enough.

3. Make a Company-Wide Commitment to Hire and Develop a Skilled, Diverse Workforce

This speaks for itself. Diversity is no longer a choice—

demographics is driving a change in the talent pool. It is not difficult to find a skilled and diverse workforce, but you do have to put strategies and tactics in place to find good candidates from any background. In case you are still wondering whether it matters, remember that diversity affects dollars!

4. Establish Strategies, Tactics, and Communication Tools toward Diversity and Inclusion

Your company should already have a strategic plan. Does it include diversity and inclusion? You already have a marketing plan. Does it include tactics to increase market share through D&I? You already have a communication plan. Does it include key messaging to reach diverse markets? All you are going to do is strengthen the plans you already have in place to make more money.

5. Implement Diversity Metrics to Measure Progress toward Inclusion

I have seen many ways to measure diversity and inclusion. Some even include mathematical equations! However, we are talking about people. You cannot measure humanity through math. Technically, you can measure diversity by how many diverse people work in your organization. For inclusion, though, you talk to people. You create employee engagement surveys, focus groups, and an environment where people will speak freely without fear.

By focusing on people instead of programming, you affect your organization organically. I am not saying that programming doesn't work, but I have seen companies put too much time into programs that don't touch people. The only way to

> **By focusing on people instead of programming, you affect your organization organically.**

build an inclusive culture is to make a great impression on your people by treating them with humanity, common courtesy, and respect.

WHEN TO CALL THE EXPERTS

After implementing the five guiding principles mentioned, you might opt to bring in a professional. At my firm, our next step is to take our clients through our D&I Diagnosis. Every company is in a different place on the D&I journey. A professional can meet you where you are.

In nearly every case, I recommend in-depth interviews. This allows the expert to diagnose where you are and where you need to go next. In my experience, a company's leaders often share an assessment of their culture that doesn't line up at all with what their employees tell me later. It's important to get an accurate understanding.

When you speak to a big chunk of an organization's personnel, you get a sense of the culture. You learn what a company is doing right and where they suck. Employees will share thoughts and experiences with a stranger long before they trust your HR person enough to take it to them. Most people are not going to risk offending or upsetting the person who signs their paycheck. Even as a third-party representative, I take great pains to be sure that employees are comfortable with me and understand that our conversation is confidential. The product of these conversations is a report that captures exactly how a company's greatest asset—its people—feel about their work environment. In some cases, it has alleviated potential lawsuits.

SMART RECRUITING

You should never be so arrogant as to think that you can go it alone and understand all the nuances within diverse groups.

Since building an inclusive culture is all about people, it is imperative that your recruiting efforts attract the right people. Consider the two main variables here—the demographics of your customer base and the demographics of the community your business serves. For the sake of your company's sustainability, you want to make sure your employees reflect these demographics.

For instance, if you own or operate a store, it's going to be important to staff the store with people who look like the people you hope to attract and who can identify with products that you hope to sell. Why? Consider this story from a few years ago.

I was out shopping and saw a new head wrap that keeps you cool while you exercise or work in the heat. From what I could tell, you wet the wrap and then tie it around your head and it makes you feel 20 degrees cooler. That sounded good to me, but before I parted with my money, I first had an important question that pertained to my hair: "Will this product turn my hair into an afro?" I wanted to ask someone who had hair texture like mine. I probably could have asked anyone in the store, but I didn't because I didn't feel like anyone would understand. Inevitably, I left the store without buying the head wrap simply because there was no one to reassure me that I wouldn't be wasting my money.

A story like this may sound discriminatory, but it is simply cultural. This is not to say that a salesperson of another race could not be knowledgeable about the product, but what I wanted to feel was trust: I wanted to identify with that salesperson and have a conversation knowing that they understood my hair texture and the problem I was hoping to avoid.

In another incident, my firm was subcontracting for a company hired by the City of Tulsa to work on Tulsa's thirty-year plan. Our job was to handle diversity communications and community engagement. My client needed to gain input for the plan during a series of community meetings. We held several of these meetings all over town with different groups in different areas. We wanted to access the Hispanic community, among others. I pride myself on staying educated about my industry, including keeping up to date on diverse groups locally and nationally. I have worked in the Hispanic community for years and know enough leaders to get things done, but you should never be so arrogant as to think that you can go it alone and understand all the nuances within diverse groups.

It was imperative that I included my Hispanic colleagues

during this process. There were serious issues happening within that community, guaranteeing that I would not be able to get these people to attend a community meeting. Oklahoma is known for writing and passing hateful laws toward diverse groups. In this case, Oklahoma lawmakers had passed HB 1804. According to the Oklahoma Policy Institute, it was the most controversial and contentious law in a decade. It enacted a series of restrictions intended to limit access to jobs and public services for undocumented immigrants and to expand the powers of state and local law enforcement to verify the legal status of those they encountered. We saw real problems for law-abiding citizens. Who carries around paperwork to prove their citizenship? I don't carry my birth certificate in my glove compartment or purse. We had actual cases in which Hispanic people were pulled over, arrested for lack of documentation, and then subsequently deported—all on their way to work. This was not common knowledge, but of course, those in the community knew what was going on. No amount of marketing was going to get a group of Hispanic people to come out to an unfamiliar meeting.

My trusted friends and colleagues informed me that the Hispanic community feared our meeting was a ploy to get them all in one room to round them up for deportation. By hiring my colleagues, however, we were able to get the Hispanic churches involved, hold meetings there, and provide the trust they needed. In addition, all of our marketing focused on providing input to make the future of Tulsa better. We learned that they didn't care about Tulsa's future, seeing as Tulsa didn't seem to give a damn about theirs. However, by changing the messaging and appealing to changing Tulsa's future for their children and grandchildren, they began to respond. Parents and grandparents wanted a better and safer Tulsa for their families. They wanted to help Tulsa be a place that cared about all its residents.

If I had been arrogant enough to think I could handle the Hispanic community without bringing in their community leaders, I would have failed. It didn't bother me that the community didn't respond to me in the same way that they responded to their church leaders. I understand that trust is earned, not given. Not only did it help us get the input we needed, but it also helped me exceed my goals for my client.

Another reason recruitment is imperative is the changing demographics. You cannot keep pulling from the same talent pool of white males. That pool is getting shallower. In the next twenty years (or fewer), minorities will be the majority. Most likely, there won't really be a majority group, especially a racial majority. We will all be people of color. As a result, your customer base will change. You will need to understand them, their needs, and lifestyles.

Do not ask one person from any diverse group to represent their entire community.

A common misconception is that it's as difficult to tap into this coveted diversity talent pool as it is to find the fountain of youth. I promise, it's not as difficult as you're making it. Yes, it may require a little more thought, but that work is invaluable. For instance, I noticed that my clients weren't doing the easy stuff like making contact with diverse student organizations at the colleges and universities where they recruit. Yet I was repeatedly told, "We just don't know where to find diverse professionals." I set out to prove my point that diverse talent wasn't the unicorn that people were making it out to be. I created a company called DiversityConneX.com, a website of diverse professionals looking for employment. Then I challenged my staff to build the largest network of diverse talent in Oklahoma—to make it a place where LinkedIn meets Match.com. After a few iterations, DiversityConneX.com has one of the best recruitment platforms on the market. It connects diverse professionals with careers, internships, and nonprofit and corporate board opportunities. The platform matches professionals with positions based on character, culture, compensation, competence, and of course diversity—while also taking the bias out of hiring by allowing a candidate to remain anonymous until a company asks for their contact information. The system even allows your HR Department to take an assessment to help them find the best employee, and it provides a fit score that ranks the best candidate first. The final product is a report that can be used as an interview dossier.

When I discovered that 50 percent of diverse individuals are less likely to be hired even with a degree, it really pissed me off. I can't imagine what the number must be for those without a degree. Our system works, and there are even more resources out there to aid companies in building a skilled and diverse workforce. Task your HR people with finding them. In the meantime, I would like to share a few strategies with you.

RECRUITMENT STRATEGIES

Partnerships

In looking for diverse professionals, partner with organizations that can provide potential candidates. Some of these include Historically Black Colleges and Universities (HBCUs) and professional organizations for African Americans, Asian Americans, Latinos, women, LGBTQ individuals, and people with disabilities. Most strong colleges and universities have robust diversity initiatives and D&I practitioners. Get to know them and their students. You may even contact sororities and fraternities.

Identify How Diversity Can Add Strength to the Talent Pool

As you assess potential candidates, think about how a candidate's diversity can help you in that role. For instance, does hiring someone from the LGBTQ community help you reach a market that you have found elusive? When you review the resume, does it show strong ties to that community?

When you interview this candidate, detail your needs and ask them if they can assist you in reaching those goals.

Build Your Professional Network

As a recruiter, HR person, or executive, you absolutely must build a diverse network. It should be representative of the people who will be instrumental in making your work environment an inclusive one. It will strengthen and enrich your personal network but will also speak volumes as you look to fulfill positions within your company. Diversity attracts diversity. Even if one of your contacts is not interested, they are going to know others through their networks and can help you find the best candidate.

Board Recruitment

I mentioned that my recruitment platform, DiversityConneX. com, also matches for nonprofit and corporate board positions. Finding diverse candidates to fill board positions is one of the top three issues for nonprofit and corporate boards, which is why it was so important to include board recruitment in our system. I sit on many boards and recognize board apathy for a number of reasons. When it comes to the task of adding diversity to boards, frustration is rampant on both sides of the conference table. Implement these best practices to get the most out of your diverse board members.

Be Upfront

During the first conversation, let candidates know what your expectations are for their board service. Diverse board members are asked to sit on many boards. Being on some boards is a job unto itself. If you are upfront, they can let you know whether they can fulfill the role.

I have seen frustration on both sides from a board who assumed that bringing on a person of color was going to help them connect with that community. He or she may not be able to help. Although we are all creatures of habit, people don't always identify with communities in which you believe they belong. Therefore, don't be scared to let your candidate know exactly what role you need them to fulfill; otherwise, you won't get what you need. They, in turn, might feel out of place among the other board members and consider it a waste of time.

Diverse Identities Are Not Homogenous

Do not ask one person from any diverse group to represent their entire community. Even if they are involved with their community, you want diverse opinions even within diverse communities. One friend of mine who is Native American is often asked, "How do Indians feel about this issue?" He reminds them that there are more than 500 tribes, and he is a citizen of one.

Allow Their Voice to Be Heard

If you have asked a candidate to serve on the board to help you represent your full constituency, allow that person to do their job. Don't turn a deaf ear on invaluable advice that can help you avoid embarrassing mistakes or communication issues. It's truly about inclusion. People hate to waste their time; they may really believe in your mission, but that doesn't mean they want to give up their time to help you meet a quota. They want to have an effect and feel valued.

RETENTION

Recruitment is only the beginning. It's much easier to recruit diverse candidates than it is to retain them. Companies spend a lot of money to train candidates, but if that new employee gets fed up and quits, your money is wasted. Here are a few things you can do to keep your diverse candidates.

Build a Mentorship Program

Like all professionals, the diverse ones also want to grow and move forward in their careers. Providing a strong mentorship program can help innovative, smart employees move in the right direction. A mentor–mentee relationship between diverse candidates and executives can provide confidence and the opportunities to assist the right candidates with advancement. The mentor will also learn valuable lessons about how diverse employees' experiences may differ from their own.

Promote Internally

As positions become available within your organization, promote internally first. Whenever this process is viable, it will engage all employees—but with a diversity and inclusion strategy attached to it, it can also provide an internal mechanism for helping the right diverse candidates rise through the ranks. And again, diversity retains diversity.

Provide Professional Development Opportunities

In my experience, diverse candidates disproportionately receive fewer professional development opportunities. Leaders often reach out to develop employees they can relate to; yet reaching out to diverse candidates internally can pay big dividends. These opportunities offer growth and skills, making employees a continued asset to your company but also engaging them enough to stay with your company.

It's not difficult to build an inclusive culture. Apply the guiding principles in this book, use surveys, and build focus groups for in-depth interviews to diagnose your company culture. You should also create strategies for attracting diverse employees and foster dialogue and an open environment where your employees provide input. Use their ideas to create organic principles that become the fabric of your operation. Remember: the focus is on people. When people feel valued, they will work hard to provide you with their best. In turn, this creates a work environment that gives your company a competitive advantage.

PERMISSION: GRANTED TO

- Confront bias for the sake of humankind. Bias is the antithesis of inclusion and humanity.

- Prioritize people. Focus on people instead of programming, knowing that people are the key to building an inclusive culture.

- Remember the facts. D&I creates a competitive advantage. I've shown you how to use my five guiding principles and other strategies. Now show your employees.

- Get down to business. Get your messaging right and recruit diverse employees who reflect the demographics your company serves to attract diverse customers. If not, you will lose customers and employees.

- Be a champion for inclusive cultures. Create an open environment of acceptance without fear. Let people share their voices—you'll be better for it.

- Stay humble. Never be so arrogant as to think you understand all diverse groups.

CHAPTER 9
ATTRACTING DIVERSE CUSTOMERS

By this point in the book, if you still do not understand why you need to attract diverse customers, you're probably a lost cause.

So, Permission: Granted to turn this book over, look out the window, and if it's a nice day, go outside and sit in the park. This book is wasting your time.

Everybody else: for the last time, it's all about the Benjamins, baby—dollar bills, y'all! Your customer base is changing as rapidly as your employee base. Are you ready for what's next? Does your marketing material reflect the changes? Do you have bilingual representatives? Is your messaging inclusive, or are you alienating particular groups?

THE REAL WHY

Demographics are the real why. Disposable buying power is the real why. Multicultural super-consumers are the real why. According to Nielsen, the U.S. multicultural buying power is growing at an exponential rate compared to the overall U.S. rate, increasing from $661 billion in 1990 to $3.4 trillion in 2014. This is more than double the growth of total U.S. buying power. In 2015, African Americans, Asian Americans, and Hispanics accounted for 38 percent of the total population. These groups are projected to grow by 2.3 million each year, reaching a U.S. minority-majority by 2044.

According to the Selig Center for Economic Growth, the total buying power in the United States was $13.5 trillion in 2015 with $3.4 trillion attributed to the top three multicultural consumer segments. That number is projected to grow to $4.2 trillion by 2020. LGBTQ buying power is near a $1 trillion as well. How much of that money did you go after? Not much, because the CMO Council and Geoscape indicated that 49 percent of senior marketing leaders did not have a multicultural marketing initiative in place. There are some states—Georgia, for instance—where African Americans hold more than a 21-percent share of all buying power in that state; $73 billion dollars, to be exact. Hispanic buying power is projected to reach $1.7 trillion for 2017.

Now how much of your budget will you earmark for multicultural marketing? What about super-consumers? They drive 30 percent of sales, 40 percent of growth, and 50 percent of the profits. Multicultural consumers disproportionately make up super-consumers in fifteen major, studied categories.[4]

As a business that is constantly searching for new customers, you should be either extremely angry at lost business or extremely excited about the opportunities by now. Remember,

4 http::www.nielsen.com/us/en/insights/news/2015/the-making-of-a-multicultural-super-consumer-html (Accessed March 10, 2017)

we are talking about disposable income—money spent on goods and services after bills are paid. Have you been leaving that money on the table? What would one percent of five trillion dollars do for your bottom line?

Many times, I am told that the only color businesses care about is green. I wish that were true, but the number of discrimination lawsuits and complaints filed yearly prove otherwise.

IMPROVING YOUR DIVERSITY COMMUNICATIONS

There are a couple of different facets to achieving better diversity communications. Improvements should be external *and* internal. External changes are what can attract diverse customers, and we'll get to those in a second. Internal changes will address communication methods inside your organization. This is specific to launching diversity and inclusion initiatives among your employees, and it is worth talking about first because I have seen it fail so many times.

INTERNAL COMMUNICATIONS

"We can no longer say Merry Christmas. Now it's Happy Holidays. This company used to represent the Christian values that I believe in."

"They only care about *millennials*. They are the future leaders of this company. What about me? I've been here twenty-five years."

"Diversity excludes white males. I can't support it. What about my sons and grandsons? They won't have jobs."

These are all real quotes from my in-depth interviews with

Imagine if everything you encountered represented someone else's life or lifestyle.

employees of Fortune 500 companies. This happens when diversity and inclusion initiatives are not communicated properly. What you are trying to accomplish for everyone can lead to (or at least imply) exclusion for some.

Of course, you will deal with some negativity or vitriol no matter what you do, especially if you are leading change, but it can be drastically reduced when you follow a process that allows employees to provide input and understand goals. For instance, you can't constantly talk about millennials as the future of your company without making sure your internal processes support all employees who seek growth inside the company they have worked so hard to build. Instead of saying, "Millennials are the future of our company," try this: "We are excited that millennials will join all our employees in leading our company into a successful future." See, it's simple. This statement allows you to let millennials know you understand what they bring to the table, but it doesn't shut out the rest of your workforce. They will hear you acknowledge the value and institutional knowledge they contribute to the company. If you change your messaging from *Merry Christmas* to *Happy Holidays*, you might use a blog post to explain to employees that *Happy Holidays* is inclusive for all employees. Merry Christmas excludes those who celebrate Kwanza, Hanukkah, or no Christmas at all. *Happy Holidays* allows all employees to feel good, not just those who are Christian. Fair-minded people will understand and embrace this language. Religious zealots will not be happy, but frankly, you should not have to explain why you want to foster an environment where certain groups within your workforce don't feel marginalized based on their belief systems. Yet you will have to explain it, anyway, because once a custom has gone on long enough, it is woven into your core values. Change is messy. It is important to take your employees through this cultural change together instead of handing down mandates. They need to be an organic part of the change. You need their input and buy-in for a successful campaign.

Outside of messaging, also missing internally is representation of your employees and customers in your marketing materials. This is getting better but it's nowhere close to normal. I know this is an external issue as well, but I'm addressing it internally because this is where the materials are produced. Any communication should reflect those it serves. Last year, Apple finally released emoticons in different shades so that all their users could identify. It may seem like it's no big deal, but unless you're blonde and fair-skinned, the old emojis just didn't feel accurate or expressive. Imagine if everything you encountered represented someone else's life or lifestyle. As a white person, what if you had to use emoticons that only represented people of color? Alternatively, what if every time

If you're uncomfortable, then you need to hire someone who isn't.

you shopped for a greeting card, you never saw white people on the front of the card? I'm left-handed. I never sat in a desk at school that allowed me to write in a comfortable position. We lefties write slanted because we don't have the same accommodations that will allow us to write as everyone else does. It doesn't seem like a big deal when you are born with those privileges. Nevertheless, if you think about it, it really starts to get on your nerves after a while. It all comes back to your in-house marketing decisions, but let me give you a tip: it's tricky. Just because you have diverse people working on the materials doesn't guarantee an inclusive final product. Habits run deeper than we know.

I didn't understand why people were so shocked by the test conducted on kids to see which doll they would choose when being presented with a white doll and a black doll. A few headlines said, "Black Kids Still Failing Doll Test." How can those kids not pick a white doll when they hardly ever see anything that represents who they are? From greeting cards to emoticons, they saw no representation. I found it easy to understand why they saw value in choosing the white doll. They felt like it was the only acceptable answer, regardless of which one looked more like them. Is that how you want your employees and customers to feel when they interact with your marketing materials?

I have a client who does a decent job of reflecting their diverse workforce in their marketing materials, but they have no representation of the employees who have a physical disability. They are worried that the employees who have a disability will receive it negatively. I understand that they don't want to single them out but their materials represent every other stripe of diversity they employ. It looks worse to exclude them; the company has employees whose daily realities are shaped by their physical differences, but its materials suggest that it doesn't value their contributions enough to show their faces on the marketing materials.

Despite its past failings, I think Walmart does a great job with this. Every circular they release uses actual employees in the pictures, and these pictures represent every group.

Our collective economic and social stability depends on inclusion.

They even use their employee's kids in the ads. This personal touch endears you to their store.

The message is simple. Do not exclude anyone for any reason. Get a diversity communications audit. Allow a professional to assist you with what my firm calls an inclusionary media campaign.

EXTERNAL COMMUNICATIONS

Are you advertising your product or service where all your potential customers are sure to see it? Have you researched the communication vehicles that your potential super-consumers are riding on? Advertising dollars spent on diverse media do not come close to matching those spent on mainstream media, not yet—according to Nielsen.com, 92 percent of the total growth in U.S. population from 2000 to 2014 is attributed to multicultural consumers. Additionally, as I said earlier, multicultural consumers disproportionately make up your super-consumers, and multicultural buying power is twice that of the country's general buying power.

Why are you not placing ads where these audiences are sure to receive your message? When exploring diverse markets, I encourage you to look beyond traditional advertising venues. Think about these things.

Attract the right customers.

Remember, don't view diverse groups as monolithic, homogenous communities. Do your research. Within a diverse community, know the age range, communication techniques, and listening and viewing habits of the people you want to attract. You need to understand consumer behavior and diverse market buying. Where are they spending money? Is it on your product or service? If so, are they spending it with you?

Know how to reach your intended audience.

Again, you have to be creative. Utilize street teams. I employ street teams to go into communities where I need to create a presence. Street teams can consist of a group of people who wear branded company t-shirts and go out to create a buzz about your product or service by talking to people in your target market and leaving behind material. Alternatively, it can just be a few people you employ to drop off your materials to popular hangouts in the community. Seek advertising and earned media opportunities in diverse publications or broadcast channels.

Do Shit Differently.

There are many ways to attract diverse markets. Dig deeper. Look for new products and market development opportunities that meet the needs of underserved segments. Have you ever thought about barbershops, beauty salons, or car shows? These places can help you to spread the word about your product or service. Go to an African American barbershop on a Saturday morning. You will immediately understand why this is an untapped way to promote your product or service. Now that you have gotten through your BS, you can think more clearly and creatively.

Hook up with partners.

We have worked with colleges and universities, barbershops, hair salons, churches—you name it. Wherever they are, you want to look for the places that are staples in diverse communities. See how your brand can be involved in the things going on in the communities that you are trying to attract.

Don't try to be too down.

I think this hurts many well-intentioned companies. We have all heard the saying, "The road to hell is paved with good intentions." Case in point: in Oklahoma, a respected eyeglass store decided to go after the African American consumer by using a popular song at the time by rapper Juvenile. The name of the song is "Back that Ass Up." You can tell this is going to be bad, right? The clean version is called "Back that Thang Up." Essentially, the commercial said, "Back that thang on up to X Store for a fresh pair of glasses." This was many years ago, but I have never forgotten that commercial because I thought it was so distasteful. I could not believe that they thought the commercial would attract people with the disposable income to spend on a pair of glasses.

The commercial was wrong on so many levels, but particularly stupid because that song was attractive to young people ages 18 to 25 (and maybe younger), not the age demo that could afford to purchase glasses with their own money. If you are not going to employ someone who is responsible for making sure your diverse marketing efforts targets the right demo, at least run it by a trusted friend or colleague from that community. Ask for an honest opinion.

Here's the thing. It is not so much that you need to do things so differently from how you would do them in the white or mainstream community; even there, you have segmented audiences. Everybody is diverse in some way. In the mainstream communities, your standard first step is to research your markets until you understand them, and then you create campaigns around your research.

The process should be the same for the diverse consumers you want to attract. However, because your head is full of BS that tells you you're unfamiliar or uncomfortable with diverse communities or people, you freak out and cut corners because it's out of your comfort zone to attend a Muslim prayer service or go to a barbershop on a Saturday. Again, these are staples of the community in diverse markets. It does not require more work—just different work. The techniques are the same. Only the nuances are different. You don't have a choice anymore. If you're uncomfortable, then you need to hire someone who isn't.

Where the United States once had a Caucasian-dominated society, today, minorities are becoming the majority. If business leaders, elected officials, and community leaders don't begin to grasp the fact that economic impact goes much deeper than pushing products, the divisiveness that consumes our nation will continue to stunt our growth as a society— especially within communities and domestic business.

OUT OF MANY, ONE

Out of Many, One is a slogan you may recognize written in Latin on our money: *E Pluribus Unum*. The concept of diversity is literally written on our money! The minds that chose our national symbols may not have been thinking about the topic of this particular book, but it is a strong point. There is only one color, which creates economic increase: green.

If successful companies understand nothing else, they understand money. They know how to monopolize it, make it, leverage it, and replenish it. They also understand how urban America can make them richer, at least as it pertains to big business. In everything—from clothing and music to cars, alcohol, and jewelry—companies have realized that a bigger market share means crossing the lines of race, ability, gender, and sexuality. Envisioning the payoff, they have had no problem with using multicultural marketing to increase their bottom lines. But, outside of these realms, diverse markets aren't valued as they should be.

As a small business owner and D&I strategist, it is my obligation to show how embracing diversity is a radical but necessary shift. No matter your race, our collective economic and social stability depends on inclusion. Besides improving business health, D&I also strengthens cities, states, and communities. Employing the same tactics used by business owners to sell products and services to diverse markets will communicate a robust and welcoming business climate—thereby increasing our population, which affects our workforce, which affects our businesses, which are the main drivers of our local economies.

Get out of your box and think differently. Attracting diverse customers is a business imperative and an enriching way to understand how America is changing. This will not only strengthen and sustain your business but will also improve your quality of life and that of those around you.

PERMISSION: GRANTED TO

- Go get that money. Tap into multicultural buying power, which is double that of the overall U.S. rate, and engage super-consumers. These actions could change the game for your business.

- Be unconventional. Look beyond traditional advertising venues, attract the right customer, know how to reach your intended audience, and develop partnerships.

CHAPTER 10

IT'S ALL BS

I know street life. I know what it is like to live in a close-knit community. I understand the corporate world and the aches and rewards of the entrepreneur.

I know what it's like when your family falls apart. I know what it is like to have a huge family, to be a big sister, to be an aunt. I understand straight and same-sex relationships and the fears that sexuality causes in society. I know what it is like to play basketball at the junior college and Division I levels; it taught me how to form a family with a group of girls I didn't know. I know what it is like to be the grandkid of a strict religious grandfather. I understand how it feels to grow up in a community that is 3 percent African American, and I know what it is like to lose someone you love either because they walked away or death interrupted the relationship. I bring all of this to the table whenever I am part of any conversation. Depending on who I am talking to, I can codeswitch my language from slang to corporate jargon to sports talk and fit myself into any scenario. Diversity is the uniqueness of who you are at the very core of your being.

That's why diversity breeds innovation.

When I sit around that table with other diverse people and we get to know each other, inclusion connects us. We form a team that will help us to reach personal and professional goals. As a result, productivity and sales rise. They rise because everyone brings diverse backgrounds, experiences, and thoughts to the process. Everyone at the table has an ownership stake in the innovation.

As we reach this final chapter, I hope you come away inspired to implement an initiative with strategies that address the well-being of the whole person. Only then can your company or organization realize the competitive advantage of diversity and inclusion.

And if your company is still trying to figure out whether diversity and inclusion should be a part of its core values, your company is in trouble. Some leaders still ask me if their business should prepare for D&I in the workplace or if it is still an issue. I always respectfully answer yes, but in my head, I'm thinking, Are you f*in' kidding me? It is here for good!

The future is now. Demographics have already changed.

Diversity breeds innovation.

Some states are already minority-majority, and this trend will continue through 2044, the year by which experts estimate the United States will be minority-majority. The new question to ask is this: Because diversity is everywhere we look—in our communities, the workplace, and our churches—how do we embrace it, create a culture of inclusion, and help everyone feel welcomed and valued?

Almost daily, the media includes a story on diversity in business. The coverage usually seems negative. These stories create a lot of upset—and in extreme cases, social upheaval. You can always count on the fact that money will be a factor in some way; either a company or a person will spend money to repair their reputation or settle a lawsuit. Diversity affects dollars. It is critical for companies to understand this, and I have a hundred ways to drive the point home for my clients.

This nation was built because of difference. However, today, in the place whose continuum spans so many ethnicities, cultures, and expressions, we are still labeling people based on appearances. It doesn't say much about how we have evolved as a people, does it? Surely, we must understand and embrace the contributions that have made the United States strong. Those contributions have come from an array of diverse individuals. It makes no sense that diversity and inclusion should be a passing phenomenon that people fail to understand. The beginning, the middle, and the end all encompass all humanity.

We cannot continue to implement diversity and inclusion initiatives as a reactive solution. D&I is a proactive strategy. Anytime something is forced, especially in response to a bad situation, it meets resistance and usually creates a hostile environment for those who blew the whistle.

I remember being forced to take my little sister with me when I went to hang out with my friends. I was angry because I did not want to take her, so I wasn't the nicest big sister. However,

I kept an eye on her and made sure she was okay only because I didn't want to meet my parents' wrath later. Decision-makers implementing diversity programs go through a transition period of feeling the exact same way—forced to do something they may deem unnecessary to the company's progress. Therefore, although the program is implemented and managed, the people affected do not feel the love and authenticity of it (trust me, my sister felt no love from me on those forced outings) so they continue to complain and feel alienated.

Why? Because there is no respect there.

Once diversity and inclusion is woven into your company's operational fabric and your own personal habits, you will begin to understand the value of diversity and how it improves your products and services. More importantly than that, you open yourself up to putting humanity first. I realized this with my sister as we got older. I did not know it then, but she was my best friend, and no one has ever had my back like she has. Of course, she was a pest—siblings are—but I am better because she is in my life. It is the same with diversity and inclusion.

I think most employees consider D&I practices a nuisance, but companies will realize that they are much better off financially and socially for embracing those concepts—especially later, when D&I becomes an economic strength.

Life would have been easier if I would have offered to take my sister on my outings with friends, just as D&I initiatives are a lot easier to implement when you're not forced to implement them because it's been mandated in a lawsuit. There are approximately 1,000 discrimination cases filed yearly in corporate America. Is that how you want to spend your profits?

The world has shifted. Long gone are the days of Dr. King's "I Have a Dream" speech, in which he envisions black and white children joining hands. It is no longer a dream. It is reality, even if some people only grudgingly admit it.

Our jobs and communities are forcing us to sit at the table together, but we still are not at a level where everyone at the table is comfortable and feels welcome. This means that we have not yet reached peak performance as a culture, a nation, or an economy.

Remember, companies that don't embrace diversity and inclusion today will miss out, but companies that don't embrace diversity and inclusion tomorrow will become obsolete.

I once heard Oprah say that the worst thing you can do to someone is make them invisible. This world and its authorities have made people feel invisible far too long. No one can live—let alone thrive—under a cloak of invisibility, unseen, unheard, and devalued. It is my goal to open up a different, more acceptable way of thinking about business and community. We do this by working on ourselves. All change starts with changing yourself first. I have repeated this theme throughout the book—it all comes down to humanity. If we can truly understand the Platinum Rule, which is to treat people as they want to be treated, then everything else falls into place. That includes economic stability.

Too simplistic for you? Think about what it has taken to induce so much pervasive mistrust and pain—all the acts against humanity. That history is what has gotten us into this situation. Surely, acts in support of humanity can get us out. We just have to stop being arrogant, unapologetic, and egotistical.

I grant you permission to feel however the hell you need to feel about issues surrounding diversity and inclusion. It's how you'll get your bias synapse in check and realize finally that it really is all bullshit.

Remember, companies that don't embrace diversity and inclusion today will miss out, but companies that don't embrace diversity and inclusion tomorrow will become obsolete.

Do not allow your corporate culture to be at odds with itself. You see the census numbers; you know that change is happening. Why not start now instead of joining the cause when it's too late?

There is no them. It is only us. All of us.

ABOUT RISHA GRANT

Risha Grant is a CEO, Author & Speaker. She founded Risha Grant LLC, an award-winning, full-service diversity communications, training and consulting firm 18 years ago. Its mission is to utilize diversity communication strategies, tactics and training as a catalyst to create inclusive cultures in companies and communities.

Risha soon realized that diversity recruitment would be a very important element of this strategy. Therefore as an ancillary product, she founded DiversityConneX.com to assist her clients in creating a diverse workforce as well as to assist nonprofits with building diverse boards.

Motivated by her passion to correct societal isms like racism, sexism, classism and plain old stupidism, it is Risha's personal mission to expose the value of Diversity & Inclusion while shining a light on the economic impact it creates. To that end, she has personally raised more than half a million dollars toward Diversity & Inclusion economic development and empowerment projects.

Using passion, persistence and knowledge to solidify a seat at the table, she has consulted with Governors, Mayors, an NBA franchise and CEO's of Fortune 500 companies and other business and community leaders to discuss and strategize Diversity & Inclusion initiatives.

For more information, call 918.581.8900 or check out our websites at www.RishaGrant.com or www.DiversityConneX.com.